COLLEGE AND THE
BLACK STUDENT

NAACP TRACT FOR THE TIMES

COLLEGE AND THE
BLACK STUDENT

NAACP TRACT FOR THE TIMES

Committee on Campus Troubles

of

The National Board of Directors

of

The National Association

for

The Advancement of Colored People

Edited by Buell G. Gallagher

with a

Foreword by Roy Wilkins

A Publication
of the
NAACP Special Contribution Fund
made possible by the generous action of
The Leonard and Sophie Davis Foundation, Inc.

The National Association for the Advancement of Colored People

1790 Broadway   New York, N. Y. 10019

$1.00 Postpaid

SPECIAL COMMITTEE ON CAMPUS TROUBLES

(Authorized July 2, 1970)

(Appointed September 15, 1970)

by

The National Board of Directors

of

The National Association

for

The Advancement of Colored People

Membership from the National Board:

Buell G. Gallagher, *Chairman*

Kenneth R. Brown   Max Delson
Vernon K. Sport   Samuel A. Williams

Staff Members:

James Brown, Jr.,   Gloster Current,
  Director, Youth and   *Director of Branches*
  College Division   June Shagaloff Alexander,
Nathaniel Jones,   *Education Director*
  General Counsel

This tract is the collective product of the Special Committee on Campus Unrest which was created by the National Board of Directors of the National Association for the Advancement of Colored People at its meeting in Cincinnati, Ohio, July 2, 1970, together with members of the National Staff.

The members of the committee assume full responsibility for what is said herein.

FOREWORD

All over America, campuses have been in turmoil. Racial injustice, and the anger of students who want justice and equality, are among the reasons for this turmoil.

No campus has a right to expect tranquility unless racism has been rejected and the campus affords full opportunity for mutual respect and affection based on justice.

Before the next round of disorders erupts, self-analysis and corrective action could remove racism from the list of causes for these troubles. This pamphlet, COLLEGE AND THE BLACK STUDENT: NAACP *Tract For The Times,* tells how.

Prepared through seven months of hard work by a special committee of the Board of Directors of the National Association for the Advancement of Colored People, under chairmanship of the dedicated and distinguished educator, Buell G. Gallagher, COLLEGE AND THE BLACK STUDENT speaks directly to the needs and problems of the campus.

Not because the situation is lacking in urgency, but because colleges are supposed to be open to the quiet voice of reason, the authors have kept their rhetoric in low key. Their soft language is not intended to deceive anyone. Students, teachers and administrators who dare to hope that, on their own campus, they still have time to achieve a society of decency and dignity without going through the counterproductive disruptions of recent years, may find in these pages the inspiration to galvanize them into action. It is apparently far later than many of us have realized.

The National Association for the Advancement of Colored People—the oldest, largest and most effective of the Civil Rights organizations—believes that there are many campuses where affirmative action will be welcome. As we thank our special committee and, particularly, Dr. Gallagher for preparing this tract, we also commend it to every campus in the nation in the hope that each will give it immediate consideration and action.

Roy Wilkins
Executive Director,
The National Association
for the Advancement of
Colored People.

New York City,
March 31, 1971.

CONTENTS

CHAPTER I

DUNGEON DOOR

Black students, as distinguished from a very small cadre of militants, want "in," not out of American society. No matter how much they may talk about separatism and nationalism and revolution, they still work hard at changing the system rather than destroying it. As one of the co-authors of "Black Power" put it in February 1969:

"They would deny this at first. But most of them don't talk in terms of developing a separate state; most of them talk of developing at their own institutions an Afro-American studies institute or black history courses. But notice they're still working with the institution. They are not saying, 'We want to throw over the university.' They're simply saying, 'We want to make it over'."

By contrast, says Charles V. Hamilton,

"The demands made by white-radical groups like SDS are generally vague and broad—working against the system—while the blacks are still working within the system. They're still very system-oriented, except they've got in mind a revised, restructured, reoriented system."[1]

These words were written by the (then) Chairman of the Department of Political Science at Roosevelt University who collaborated with Stokely Carmichael in writing "Black Power." They were written after the murder of Dr. Martin Luther King, Jr., had reportedly dampened the ardor of black youth, supposedly substituting cynicism for idealism and alienating them from the (white) Establishment.

There had been a time when white and black youth had struggled —and died—together in the cause of non-violent social change. Throughout the South, they integrated public facilities and fought for integrated schools and colleges. And when many of the whites moved on to other causes—Free Speech, Peace, Clean Environment, Women's Liberation—black youth stubbornly clung to its own Thing: racial justice, racial identity, racial empowerment. As white youth shifted its arena from the Deep South to the northern campus, black youth found itself embattled on scores, yes hundreds, of campuses throughout the nation; but the interracial coalition of the early 1960s was no longer cemented by common interest and shared goals.

[1] *Newsweek*, Feb. 10, 1969. (Hamilton is now at Columbia University.)

1

Black youth began to go it alone. To the superficial observer, it began to seem that black youth had abandoned the fight for integration. They had not. They had merely drawn on strength where it could be found, namely, from within the group.

Nevertheless, a new rhetoric became fashionable. "The black revolutionary nationalist," said Nathan Hare (San Francisco State College), "aware and proud of his blackness, demands the right to exist as a distinct category, to be elevated as such by any means necessary."[2]

As Hare pointed out, this posture was assumed largely because the white colleges were dominated by "various shades of racist persuasions." Separatism, and especially the rhetoric and vehemence of it, can best be interpreted as a revolt against the complacency of white racism in a culture and country which have long protested innocence of such racism. "For black children crippled by defeatist attitudes, hardened by generations of exclusion,"[3] the separatist point of view claims to be the road to self-respect, ethnic identity and racial pride.

There are times when emotion and sentiment and anger run stronger than reason and logic. This may be one of those times.

But not necessarily so. Certainly, not inevitably so. There is another way. To those for whom Roy Wilkins speaks, separatism becomes "simply another exercise in racial breastbeating."[4] In fact, it is "the door to a dungeon." And the closed door, which shuts out the white, also shuts the black in.

There are those who argue that the militant demands of the separatists are mainly rhetoric, not actually intended to be taken literally. They cite, for example, the recent utterances of Stokely Carmichael, who in 1971 claims to have moved beyond his earlier sloganeering, saying, "The time of entertainment is over." As reported in the *New York Times*,[5] he appears to have abandoned the call for black revolution within the United States in order to espouse a movement for world revolution—shifting the emphasis from Black Power within the United States to African domination of the world. "We must build Mother Africa," he now says, and from that continental base build the new revolution. "Yes, America will be destroyed; but we must not be destroyed with America."

Whether Carmichael's new tack, and the disintegration of the formerly solid front of Black Panther leadership, taken together, can be said to indicate that the militancy of black separatism has run its course, is a question only the future can answer. We are here concerned with both the rhetoric and the tactics of black separatism on the American campus. Where is it likely to lead? What vitality does it have? What

[2] ibid.
[3] ibid.
[4] ibid.
[5] March 21, 1971

2

are its short-run effects? And what results may be expected over the long haul?

The quick answer is this: *Black students have the right to claim their own identity, to live in institutions which let them control their own lives and find their own meanings, to be men and women in their own right. They are going to exercise these rights—now! And if separatism is the only door opened for the realization of these rights, the presently recognized black student leadership is going to use that door, and slam it behind themselves.* They will enjoy wall-to-wall freedom within the dungeon; but, at least within those limits, they will be free to do as they choose.

There is another answer. *Self-respect and ethnic identity and racial pride could be achieved within a multi-racial society if the struggle for equality, justice, freedom and brotherhood were not abandoned. Only in an open society can the true value of each man and women and each child be secure, despite—and because of—racial identity. Achieved in separatism, racial pride is nothing but a black copy of white racism.*

The early leaders of the black student movement in the 1960s saw this truism. They were deeply religious, integrationist, believing intensely in cooperation between blacks and whites, espousing non-violence. But the long hot summers of Freedom Rides and Freedom Marching—plus the slowness of results—changed all that. The Student Non-violent Coordinating Committee retained its SNCC acronym, but "Non-violent" became "National," as a logical development of the newly vigorous Black Nationalism. One after the other, formerly inter-racial civil rights movements lost (or expelled) their white membership and became racially chauvinistic, in part as a response to the wave of black rage which swept the country and erupted in urban riots. Among the civil rights organizations, only the Urban League and the National Association for the Advancement of Colored People escaped the full effects of the new bitterness of black youth in the late 1960s.

For, among that youth, instant idealism had led not to instant success but to instant disillusionment. The task of the 1970s is to rediscover the deeper and continuing meanings of an idealism for which a great succession of leaders and followers have laid down their lives, and to redouble our flagging efforts to realize those ideals.

The chapters which follow trace the beginnings of the fight for the educational rights of Negroes in the efforts which, among other things, made it possible for the new breed of black student leadership to emerge. In these chapters, some misguided leadership (usually white and liberal) on northern campus is exposed as having mistakenly believed that the new demands could be met (or parried) with moderate and paternalistic adjustments. Other leadership (usually militant and black) is exposed as playing into the hands of segregationists by espousing the New Separatism in a form which compromisingly accommodates

3

Jim Crow. Several chapters deal with the sweeping campus reforms and restructuring which are essential to relevance, in the belief that the academic establishment (both white and black) can become an instrument of constructive purpose rather than a defense of decadence. The final chapter and the Appendix provide a few tools for institutional self-analysis which should be useful in the continuing struggle.

CHAPTER II

THE LAW, THE COURTS AND THE CONSTITUTION

The Constitution of these United States, while based on the assertion that all men are created equal, was signed by men who agreed that a slave was only three-fifths equal. It took a civil war to change that agreement and to amend the Constitution so that it affirmed that every man counted as a whole man. It has taken a century of conflict to get the laws and the courts of the nation to agree with the 13th, 14th and 15th amendments.

The nadir in that century of struggle was the verdict of the United States Supreme Court in *Plessy v. Ferguson* (1896), a case in which the court decided that blacks could be segregated in separate cars on the railroad without doing violence to the constitutional rights of anyone—provided only that the accommodations for the two races were equal.

In the wake of that decision, many states hastened to provide "separate but equal" accommodations everywhere and to make it illegal for either race to use the facilities reserved for the other. The deaf, dumb and blind were segregated by color. White nurses were forbidden to take care of black males. In South Carolina, black and white cotton workers were forbidden to look out of the same window. Florida required textbooks destined for use by black pupils to be separated from those intended for whites while the books were still in the warehouse. Jim Crow Bibles were provided and prescribed for oath-taking by witnesses in court cases. Hospitals, libraries, drinking fountains, railroad cars and waiting rooms, dining and pullman cars, theatres, hotels, restaurants—everything in life available for use by the public was segregated by color. And when he died, the black man went to a racially segregated cemetery. These practices were enshrined in custom and imbedded in law. They had the full support of the courts, legislators and state and local governments in the seventeen segregating states. They were not seriously challenged outside the South. And, of course, colleges and universities were among the segregated institutions.

This is not the place to trace the whole history of the fight to bring the full force of the law, the courts and the Constitution to bear upon Jim Crow and banish him from the nation. It is necessary, however, to understand what has happened with reference to colleges and universities in the eyes of the law and the Constitution, if we are to understand the present crisis on campus.

5

Begin the story with the *Gaines* case. Lloyd Gaines was a Negro who in 1935 had been refused admission to the law school of the University of Missouri solely because of his race. He brought legal action to compel the university to admit him, claiming as he did so that refusal to grant admission was a denial of the equal protection clause of the Fourteenth Amendment. The registrar urged him to accept a scholarship to some law school outside the state—at least until such time as Missouri established a Negro law school within its boundaries. The state would even pay his tuition to that other law school if he would go there. Gaines replied that he wanted to go to law school in his own home state; and, more importantly, he claimed that the State of Missouri could not avoid its constitutional obligation to provide the "equal protection" which the 14th Amendment required.

The Missouri Supreme Court dismissed that argument and dismissed the case. But the National Association for the Advancement of Colored People had been providing the legal counsel for Mr. Gaines, and now NAACP attorneys Charles H. Houston and S. R. Redmond appealed to the United States Supreme Court. There, the decision was reversed on the narrow ground that the Constitution required the State of Missouri to provide equal facilities for Negroes *within* the state, and in the absence of such facilities it had to admit applicants to the *existing* University of Missouri Law School. Forty-two years after *Plessy v. Ferguson,* the Supreme Court took the first short step away from the doctrine of separate-but-equal, by asserting that if there were no separate accommodations provided by the State, then clearly, since *nothing* cannot be equal to *something,* Mr. Gaines was being denied "equal protection" of the laws in Missouri. That was in 1938. The Fourteenth Amendment had been part of the Constitution for seventy years. Now, for the first time, it was directly applied by the court to higher education.

The NAACP brought a long succession of suits in behalf of clients suing for admission to southern all-white institutions and basing their suits on the equal protection clause. For example, a decade after *Gaines v. Missouri,* Miss Ada Lois Sipuel, a black woman, was denied admission to the law school of the University of Oklahoma. Attorneys of the NAACP, Thurgood Marshall and Amos Hall, petitioned in the Oklahoma courts for an order directing her admission. The State of Oklahoma contended that the *Gaines* decision did not require a state wherein segregation laws were in effect to admit a black person to its white schools. Furthermore, the Oklahoma court held that there was no obligation on the part of the State of Oklahoma to set up a law school for Negroes unless Negroes who desired a legal education in Oklahoma first requested that a school be set up. The Supreme Court of Oklahoma upheld the decision of its lower court, denying Miss Sipuel's plea. But the Supreme Court of the United States, on appeal, held that the meaning of its decision in the *Gaines* case was that the State had to provide a law school for blacks just as soon as it provided one for whites. And one month later, in the case of *Fisher v. Hurst*, the Supreme Court went one step further when it held that, while waiting for a black law school to be established, the State had to admit a Negro applicant into the existing law school—unless it stood ready to refuse all white applicants as well. Things were beginning to move.

But there was still a long way to go. Professor G. W. McLaurin, an Oklahoman and black, decided that he wanted to get his doctorate from the public university in his home state. Under the protection of the court decisions in *Gaines, Sipuel* and *Fisher*, since the state did not provide a doctoral program for blacks, Mr. McLaurin was admitted to the all-white graduate school. But Oklahoma had segregation statutes. So, McLaurin sat at a separate desk, in an anteroom, where he could see and hear the professor through an open door without being seen by other students. He sat only at a designated desk on the mezzanine floor of the library, and ate his meals only at a special table in the cafeteria and at different times from all other students. When nation-wide public criticism was brought to bear, this extreme situation was modified, without being corrected: he could sit inside the classroom, but only in a row of chairs labeled "colored." His library seat was moved to the main floor but still separately assigned; he could eat his meals at the same time as all others, but only at his own special and separate table. He *could* stand in the same line at the cafeteria, use the same corridors and stairways, and actually draw out from the library the same books as other students! When the Supreme Court took a good look at the absurdities of this segregation, it moved a little farther along the road toward sanity, saying:

"We conclude that the conditions under which (McLaurin) is required to receive his education deprive him of his personal and present right to the equal protection of the laws.

"We hold that under these circumstances the 14th Amendment precludes differences in treatment by the state based upon race. (McLaurin) having been admitted to a state-supported graduate school, must receive the same treatment at the hands of the state as students of other races."

Mr. McLaurin was now free to be a man in the graduate school of his own home state.

Other states got the message. There was a scramble to establish instant law schools and instant graduate schools for Negroes throughout the seventeen segregating states. But it was too late. In Texas, for example, where a separate law school had been set up for a handful of black students including Heman Sweatt, a suit was brought to force the state to drop its subterfuge and open its authentic law school.

7

Sweatt sued, and NAACP lawyers argued his case. In an opinion written by the late Chief Justice Fred M. Vinson, a Kentuckian, the Supreme Court declared:

"This court has stated unanimously that 'The state must provide (legal education) for (petitioner) in conformity with the equal protection clause of the 14th Amendment and provide it as soon as it does for applicants of any other group.

"In accordance with (decided cases) petitioner may claim his full constitutional right: legal education equivalent to that offered by the state to students of other races. Such education is not available to him in a separate law school as offered by the state."

With these words, the stage was set for the historic decision in the *Brown* case. It was now clear that there was but one way to assure equal protection of the laws, and that was to provide equal educational facilities; but the question now became: can the separate be equal?

The real test, and the real answer were to be provided in connection with the lower schools. Suits were brought on appeal to the United States Supreme Court from four states and the District of Columbia, challenging the assertion that a segregated school (elementary or high school) could be equal to a non-segregated school. The "flagship" of this "convoy" of cases turned out to be *Brown v. Board of Education* (Topeka, Kansas). The court had said that the Constitution required the states to treat all persons equally and to protect them in this equality. It had said that various devices improvised by the segregating states under pressure of the court's ruling were, in fact, evasions. It had therefore required the states to open up previously all-white campuses to enrollment by both races. In its 1954 decision it now declared that the very fact of segregation denoted inequality: dual systems must be ended.

"In these days, it is doubtful that any child may reasonably be expected to succeed in life if he is denied the opportunity of an education. Such opportunity, where the state has undertaken to provide it, is a right which must be made available to all on equal terms.

"We come then to the question presented: Does segregation of children in public schools solely on the basis of race, even though the physical facilities and other 'tangible' factors may be equal, deprive the children of the minority group of equal educational opportunities? We believe that it does.

"We conclude that in the field of public education the doctrine of 'separate but equal' has no place. Separate educational facilities are inherently unequal."

8

The court therefore directed that dual school systems be dismantled "with all deliberate speed," and sent the cases back to the lower courts for appropriate action.

Some states and localities complied at once. In other states, massive resistance was mounted. Nullification and interposition became battle cries of politicians. Governors Wallace in Alabama and Barnett in Mississippi symbolically interposed their bodies between Federal forces and state-required segregation by "standing in the school house door" to block the entrance of black applicants or Federal marshals. The agencies which monitored the public school and college situation in the formerly segregating states reported painfully slow progress. Two successive presidents of the United States brought troops into action to compel compliance and to protect integrating students from the wrath of white supporters of segregation. Some federal judges refused to move resolutely forward, out of their own uncertainty as to the meaning of the phrase "all deliberate speed." Progress, such as it was, was slow, irregular, spasmodic, ephemeral. In not a few instances, local state authorities began to believe that obduracy could transform "all deliberate speed" into "never." Finally, fifteen years after the *Brown* decision, the Supreme Court spoke again in the matter, scrapped the "all deliberate speed" instruction, and called for the *immediate* elimination of dual school systems, root and branch, wherever they existed. The Executive Branch of the Federal Government is currently claiming substantial compliance with this latest order of the court, while national educational organizations and civil rights agencies (especially the NAACP) sharply question these governmental claims.

Even so, two things are crystal clear: (1) it is contrary to the Constitution of the United States to establish or to continue, on any campus of a public college or university, any separation, segregation, or other form of distinction or discrimination based on race or color; and (2) private colleges and universities which receive federal funds are similarly under legal compulsion not to segregate or otherwise discriminate or distinguish on the basis of race, on pain of losing the federal funds.

This second development has come about with the passage of the Civil Rights Act of 1964. This was the long-awaited action by Congress, authorized by the 14th Amendment in 1868 and acted upon by Congress ninety-six years later. As the Supreme Court had said about the meaning of the Constitution, the Congress now said by legal enactment: no person may be denied the benefits of, or be subjected to discrimination because of race or color under, any program or activity receiving Federal financial assistance. Federal agencies are directed by this law to issue rules and guidelines that assure nondiscrimination in all programs receiving Federal aid. Segregation is one form of discrimination: it violates this law.

Nevertheless, some black students (principally in northern univer-

sities and colleges) and some white administrators (also mainly north-
erners) have tried to set up segregated dormitories, housing or eating
facilities at predominantly white campuses. In some instances, there
have also been efforts to establish separate departments, even colleges
or schools within a university, from which whites were to be excluded,
either as instructors or as students or both. All of these measures are
clear violations of the Constitution of the United States and of the
Civil Rights Act of 1964.

Under Title VI of the 1964 Act, college administrators are required
to take affirmative action to see to it that, as their institutions are de-
segregated in compliance with the 14th Amendment and court rulings,
they are not resegregated in any manner. The whole weight of the
law, the courts and the Constitution now bears down hard in support
of the prophetic words written by Mr. Justice Harlan in dissenting
from his colleagues on the high bench in the case of *Plessy v. Ferguson*,
that

> "Our constitution is color blind . . . The thin disguise of equal
> accommodations . . . will not mislead anyone."

In 1896, that was the lonely voice of dissent. In 1954, it became the
unanimous word of the high court. In 1964, it became the voice of
Congress. It remains to make it the way of life of the American people
and a dominant belief and practice on the American campus.

CHAPTER III

THE FORMERLY WHITE CAMPUS

During the second half of the 1960s, the nation's predominantly white campuses found themselves suddenly placed under great pressure to give dramatic demonstration to the reality of their commitment to racial justice. These pressures came from a variety of sources, including the impact of court decisions and legislation reviewed in the preceding chapter.

Many campuses throughout the North and West had for some time been pursuing, in leisurely and good-natured fashion, the goal of "better race relations" based in "equity." By the middle 1960s, the sweep of events began to dictate a quicker time-table and to demand affirmative effort far beyond that which most predominantly white campuses had as yet exerted.

As the decade ended, the tempo of history had accelerated. Student protests and campus unrest (something more than polite petitioning) occurred on 232 campuses in the spring semester of 1968-1969. Although other issues, such as the Vietnam War or parietal rules, were often present, most (59 per cent) of these campus incidents were sparked by the issue of "Black recognition" in one form or another. The specific issues, which were usually presented as "non-negotiable demands," were present in incidents of campus disturbance as follows:

Percent of 232 campus incidents in which issue was present	Issue
59%	"Black recognition" in any form
32%	"Provide more courses in Black Studies"
24%	"Increase numbers of black students"
23%	"Hire more black faculty and staff"
15%	"End discrimination and honor blacks"
9%	"Provide more facilities for black students"
8%	"Increase black representation on general committees"
4%	"Support off-campus Black Power"
4%	"Hire black employees"

Source: *Report* of the President's Commission on Campus Unrest, 1970, page 109.

The tactics and strategy of student protest over these issues of "Black recognition" on campus ranged all the way from peaceful demonstration to disruption, terrorism, takeover, kidnapping and arson. The re-action from college administrators and civil authorities ranged all the way from eager capitulation to violent repression involving death.

But these campus incidents did not occur in a vacuum. The background was provided by the volcanic eruptions of violence in northern urban centers over the preceding years. Riots of major magnitude began in Harlem and Rochester in 1964, went on to Watts in 1965, to Chicago and Cleveland in 1966, to Tampa, Cincinnati, Atlanta, Newark and Detroit in 1967, and throughout these years spilled over into satellite storms of social change in numerous incidents in smaller population centers. Campus patterns of protest over racial matters were strongly affected by the riot syndrome of the cities—both in pattern and in personnel.

The *Report* of the National Advisory Commission on Civil Disorders (March 1, 1968) found that the urban riots of the 1960s had been characterized by rumor-triggering incidents, by widespread looting and burning (which most whites condemned as criminal acts and some blacks justified as massive uprisings against an oppressive white Establishment). The Commission also found that the disorders varied widely in the degree of violence and of property damage, that they were not rightly to be interpreted as attempts to subvert or to overthrow the established American social order; that, instead, "the rioters appeared to be seeking . . . fuller participation in the social order and the material benefits enjoyed by the majority of American citizens."[1] Most significantly for the purposes of this present narrative, the Commission found that the typical leaders of the urban riots of the 1960s were not hoodlums, habitual criminals, or "outsiders." Neither were they among the less well-educated or the socially insensitive. Instead said the Commission, the typical riot leader "was a teenager or young adult, a life-long resident of the city in which he rioted, a high school drop-out—he was, nevertheless, somewhat better educated than his non-rioting Negro neighbor, and was usually underemployed or employed in a menial job. He was proud of his race, extremely hostile to both white and middle-class Negroes and, although informed about politics, highly distrustful of the political system."[2]

Although no comprehensive nation-wide survey has been conducted in the matter, it was not improbable that if a survey were to have been conducted during the recent years of campus protest, it would have shown that the typical black leader of campus protest was the collegiate counterpart of his colleague in the urban riots. Indeed, some of the campus protest leaders had themselves been participants in or sympathizers with the riots in their own home com-

[1] *Report* of the National Advisory Commission on Civil Disorders, March 1, 1968. p. 4.
[2] *Report* of the National Advisory Commission on Civil Disorders, March 1, 1968. p. 4.

munities between 1964 and 1967. Thus, in 1968 and 1969, as college matriculants, they followed the patterns of social action already learned back home—and in not a few instances, well-meaning white administrators had deliberately recruited new waves of entering blacks from the very ghettoes in which riots had occurred.

Prior to 1960, most black students on white campuses had been content to be seen, not heard (except within their own peer group). They were rarely involved deeply in campus social life, were generally excluded from membership in social fraternities and sororities and from many of the honor societies, often discriminated against in off-campus housing. Black athletes were the exception: vigorously recruited and given lucrative "scholarships" to play football, basketball or baseball or compete in track and field, the black athlete could be a Big Man on Campus (within limits) if he cared to; but he tended to consider his campus sojourn as a prelude to later professional success, and therefore he seldom found time or desire to become involved in campus activities—except that he might join one of the black social fraternities which had been created in response to white exclusiveness.

But during the 1960s a new breed of black collegian emerged. At first, he was a participant in the Civil Rights efforts in the South: the Sit-ins, Freedom Rides, Freedom Marches, Wade-ins, Pray-ins—commonly committed to nonviolence as the method and integration as the goal. Increasingly, he became disillusioned over the slow pace of school desegregation, southern resistance to the extension of voting rights and the exercise thereof, the tardy response of the Federal Government to the continued denial of equal access to public accommodations in the South, the prolongation of discrimination in employment and housing throughout the country, and his own uneasy ambivalence as a black man on a campus which was serenely content with its white self-image. He saw James Meredith entering the University of Mississippi only when the National Guard had been federalized to make the groves of academe safe for him. He witnessed the murder of Medgar Evers, shot to death as he stood in the doorway of his own home, and the death by bombing of four little girls in a Birmingham Baptist Church. He learned of the brutal murders of three young civil rights workers in Philadelphia, Mississippi—Michael Schwerner, Andrew Goodman and James E. Chaney. He saw (and followed) Martin Luther King, Jr. in Albany (1962), Birmingham (1963), Selma (1965), and Chicago (1966)—climaxed by his murder on a Memphis balcony (1968). He saw and heard a new life-style in Malcolm X, former disciple of Elijah Muhammad, outspoken champion of black nationalism, publicly murdered in 1965—and in the martyred Malcolm he found a new ideological hero.

Implicit in the black student experience of the decade was a growing disenchantment with the white Establishment—not merely the

13

old effort to get a fair share out of the American Way of Life; but, increasingly, a rejection of that way of life *per se*. This disenchantment began in disappointment, escalated through dissent, defiance and despair to disruption and destruction. It was given great emotional potency, at the same time that it was intellectually weakened, by the paradoxical demand both for complete acceptance and for complete separation. An early expression of this emerging paradox was the speech prepared by John Lewis of SNCC for delivery at the March on Washington in 1963. Even after the deletion of its censored opening paragraph, the speech still went on to say:

> "The Party of Kennedy is also the Party of Eastland.
> "The Party of Javits is also the Party of Goldwater.
> "Where is our Party?" [3]

And although Martin Luther King's "I Have A Dream" was the high point of the 1963 March, the next half-dozen years were to see disenchanted black young Americans turn away from that dream in disillusionment and bitter cynicism. "Black Power!" became the new rallying cry—the more effective because it was undefined. Quickly, "Black" became to them synonymous with the sentiments of dignity, self-identity, race consciousness and race pride. It soon began to demand the denigration of "White" as a logical (and emotionally necessary) corollary. Interracial amity came to be denounced as treasonous betrayal. Black caucuses were developed within religious, labor and other organizations. Black students' groups sprang into being on campus.

A proliferation of black student organizations, black student unions, Afro-American societies and similarly named groups (some named in Swahili) appeared almost simultaneously on hundreds of campuses. Some students and some faculty members, as minority group members in a less than affirmatively congenial white society, felt lost. They began to express a yearning for "black identity," and a concern to eliminate racial discrimination on campus—and in this double objective, embodied the paradox which was to plague the movement.

Central to the new Black Student Movement were the values of self-respect and black identity and the implied corollary—for them— of contempt for whites. These values were expressed in ever sharper and more defiant demands, on the white-controlled campus; and in changed life-style and dress, with a new evaluation of food, hairstyle, language, music, art—the works. Increasingly, the Black Movement became a means of escape toward separatism—yet, at the same time it demanded acceptance and admission into the larger society. In many instances, the black student groups saw their role as being

---

[3] "Speeches by the Leaders" in "The March on Washington for Jobs and Freedom." August 28, 1963. Printed as a public service by the NAACP.

something more than protest, something larger than self-interest. They developed projects of service to the surrounding community: here and there, failing students were tutored, hungry children got breakfast, day care centers were manned, and "liberation schools" were started. Alongside these practical expressions of compassion and concern, the Movement also produced a new level of escalated rhetoric, in some instances verging on fantasy.

Organizational patterns of these student organizations are somewhat similar, from campus to campus, although there is no central source of direction and control—not even a mailing list. Usually, incoming freshmen are recruited into membership, by a variety of methods of persuasion and pressure, including, where feasible, initial contacts with prospective students before the college year opens. In some instances, a black student group has been given authority and responsibility to recruit freshmen and to be in charge of their orientation. Experience with this device is uneven. On one campus, where there is a long tradition of commonly accepted values, together with an educational process calculated to turn out graduates to embody the values espoused by Alma Mater, the black upperclassman will, by definition, be one who will manage to recruit others like himself, namely, those who will readily accept and fit into the established patterns of the college. But at another institution, where the self-image of the undergraduate is diffuse and unfocused, the educational process is eclectic and controversy is valued above conformity, the black upperclassman will, by definition, be free to select whatever kind of prospective freshman he desires. And especially on those campuses where the cadre of black students not only recruits but also carries out the orientation of black freshmen, the predictable result is that most black freshmen are indoctrinated rather than oriented, and the rest are intimidated. The net result is disquieting in the short run and over the long haul the practice will amount to institutional suicide.

Nevertheless, many successful efforts at recruitment have been carried on, wherein both the black students (and their organizations) and the regular institutional admissions officers work together. Where the participants are attuned to the meaning and needs of the black community and know how to enlist the affirmative assistance of Negro fraternal and religious and civic groups in the recruiting exercise, black student involvement can be a plus factor.

In later chapters, subjects other than recruitment and admissions are discussed. This one topic is touched on at this point merely to illustrate the significance of the black student organization on campus.

The black student organizations have played a central part in promoting campus unrest and carrying out campus protests. Frequently they have resisted efforts of white students and white organizations to co-opt them. They have also frequently opposed white student organizations which attempted to work for racial justice on campus, saying (as an extreme instance), "Whitey, if you want to help me, then remember John Brown and be like him. And if you won't be like John Brown, then get out of my way!"

As early as 1964, a study conducted by William Brink and Louis Harris showed that 22 per cent of rank-and-file Negroes and 25 per cent of non-South slum dwellers had come to believe that some violence was inevitable, because peaceful non-violent efforts to achieve racial justice did not pay off. The murder of Dr. Martin Luther King, Jr., on April 4, 1968, was the ultimate insult to idealism, the final defeat of King's "Dream," the trigger for a nation-wide moment of black anger, riots, looting, burning, frenzied retaliatory striking out against whatever "enemy" was close at hand to be struck. Among these "enemies" was the college campus, with its white administrators and teachers and students.

Profound shock, dismay, disbelief and anger characterized the reaction of many a white campus when it was accused of being "the enemy," embodying institutional racism. By the late 1960s, most college and university presidents and faculties had become accustomed to being attacked by various student and faculty forces, as the Berkeley Syndrome spread across the nation; but very few campuses were prepared for the onslaught of black rage. Quite the contrary, a great many campuses were sincerely and vigorously at work in what they conceived to be an honest effort to make their institutions more appealing and more useful to Negro high school graduates. Ironically, it was precisely on the campuses where greater progress had been made toward better race relations that the new ebullience of black consciousness broke out in more severe protest. Exceptions prove the rule. And no northern or western or southern campus appears to have moved fast enough to merit the unqualified endorsement of the new black leadership in the student body.

The responses of white faculty and administrators in the northern and western institutions were not uniform. On the negative side of the ledger go most of the reactions from both extremes: either a condescending readiness to grant every wish the moment a black student uttered it, or the flat rejection of every demand because it came from a Negro. The positive items are less easily summarized.

Among the institutions, those which were soft-hearted-and-soft-headed found themselves approving the resegregation of black students in separate dormitories under the guise of curing individual isolation and helping to build Black Identity; establishing segregated curricula and courses of study often leading to a separate degree and having inferior academic standards, as an ill-considered response to the demand for full recognition of Black Culture and Heritage; and sometimes throwing away academic standards in order no longer to appear to discriminate against those who (as a result of slum schooling) were poorly prepared either for entrance or for continuance in college.

16

These institutions, in reality, helped black students to find the dungeon door.

The hard-headed-and-hard-hearted among the institutions found themselves rejecting grievances even when they were justified, and welcoming the intervention of political and military forces to repress campus disruption and intimidate rebellious students. The quiet on these campuses is ominous.

A few institutions appear to have been hard-hearted-and-soft-headed: they deserved what they got.

It remains for a series of institutions to discover the fruitful and hopeful answers which might be supplied by the combination of the soft heart and the hard head, responding with intelligence *and* empathy not only to the demands but also to the unarticulated needs of *all* students, including blacks.

Meanwhile, the general picture changes rapidly, while remaining much the same as it changes. In the second half of the 1960s, enrollment of black students in American higher education more than doubled, increasing from 234,000 in 1964 to 492,000 in 1969, a growth of 110 per cent.[4] Enrollment of white students in the same period increased by only 5 per cent. Nevertheless, at the end of this growth, we went into the 1970s with the ratio of college attendance by whites of college age standing at more than twice the ratio prevailing among blacks. If you are black, your chances of getting into college—let alone graduating—still are less than half as good as those of a white child.

Moreover, if you are black, the chances of your finding a favorable faculty image are not good. To be sure, the number of Negroes holding the doctorate is much lower, in proportion to their total population, than is the ratio of whites. It is also true that conscientious northern and western administrators have hesitated to "raid" the faculties of the predominantly black institutions, lest the latter be unduly weakened. Such administrators need to give some consideration also to the growing numbers of black students on their own campuses, and to reflect on the self-image such black students get when they arrive to find a black faculty representation which is small potatoes and few to the hill. Since there is a real shortage of Negro Ph.D.s and since it takes several years to produce new doctors, there will be no instant remedy to this shortage. It is true, however, that in many fields there are holders of the doctorate who are white and are unemployed due to economic conditions and the phasing out of space- and military-related industry. Some of these might be re-tooled and re-educated so as to become effective teachers on the predominantly Negro campuses, where they could relieve blacks whose presence on the predominantly white campuses is sorely needed. About the only things that seem certain on this issue at the moment are these: controversy

4 *New York Times,* Oct. 10, 1970.

will continue; black students will continue to demand more than is possible; and white administrators will continue to do less than is possible.

Finally, if you are a black student and expect to enter a college or university other than one of the traditionally Negro colleges of the South, and you would hope to find that the college of your choice is headed by a black man or woman—forget it. Aside from a few of the two-year colleges, there is only one of the predominantly white institutions in the nation that has a black president: Michigan State University, whose president is Clifton Wharton.

Colleges and universities which have, up to the present time, been predominantly white ought not to show surprise when black students protest against racism on campus. Only when "predominantly white" ceases to imply "dominated by whites" will the American campus deserve to be free from protests and disruption over the lingering presence of the legacy of the "peculiar institution" of slavery.

The most important word—and the most difficult to speak without being misunderstood or misinterpreted—has been reserved until last: *the spirit, expressed through action, finally determines results.*

The difficulty with stating this truth is that sometimes, all too often, a pronouncement of good intentions is deliberately substituted for action (as when a church body passes a resolution and then sits back and does nothing, or institutional policy is revised and little is done to implement new policy). Equally venal is that inaction which accompanies new language not because inaction is planned, but because action is not planned. In short, there are times when the declaration of brotherhood becomes the worst enemy of justice and equality. Therefore, merely to insist on the spirit of human brotherhood is to run the risk of settling for something much less than equality and justice and mutuality and decency, and therefore to betray brotherhood itself. Hence, it is sometimes thought to be better not to mention or to stress the importance of attitude, lest a change only in attitude—nothing else —occurs.

Nevertheless, the truth is that without the spirit of brotherhood, only partial justice can be obtained, inequalities will persist, and the full flowering of natural and unembarrassed affirmative affection across race lines will not come. This is true because, in a caste-structured society, all institutions and most individuals, on both sides of the caste of color, inevitably carry the taint of caste within them. Thus, whatever progress tends to come turns out to be false and ephemeral: it comes because white condescension approves it and black humiliation accepts it, or, it comes because black arrogance wrenches it from a guilt-laden white conscience. The new birth of freedom, either for the white or for the black, will not be an automatic creation of the new spirit: the millenium will not be delivered with the morning milk.

Yet, without a new spirit, the new day dies aborning.

That is why the spirit of the campus is of vital importance. All the steps advocated in this tract may be taken, but if they are taken without a meeting of the minds and spirits of both castes in an united effort— the glad release of the new spirit—normal human relationships will not follow: the caste of color will persist. But, with this spirit, carried out in practice, the campus becomes a new society, foreshadowing the future it seeks to create.

CHAPTER IV

COLLEGES FOUNDED FOR NEGROES

Two armies of occupation moved into the South following the Civil War. The Freedmen's Bureau (actually, a bureau within the War Department, called "Bureau of Freedmen, Refugees and Abandoned Lands") was created by Congress in 1865, for one year. Partly because President Andrew Johnson angered the Congress by attempting to kill the Bureau, its life was extended until 1872. During those seven years, the Bureau had a profound effect upon the South and upon race relations therein. Possessed of very broad powers over ex-slaves, it was also empowered to redistribute confiscated lands. It distributed rations and medical supplies, regulated labor contracts, administered justice in all cases involving blacks, and—most importantly—established schools and colleges for former slaves. This last function was performed both by direct action of the Bureau itself, and by giving encouragement and aid to religious organizations and benevolent societies in the founding of schools and churches for freedmen.

The Freedmen's Bureau was therefore accompanied by a second occupying force—voluntary and missionary, an "Army in Petticoats," which was recruited mainly from the Northern churches. These New Englanders had a sense of mission: to demonstrate that blacks were the equal of whites in educational potential and achievement. With this advocacy of equality they also defended freedom for the freedman. Frequently, indeed almost universally, these early colleges and schools were founded in response to the initiative of freedmen residing in the area where the institution was started up. Thus, it can be said that the initial impetus for founding and maintaining colleges for Negroes in the South was a desire to attain, and to justify in practice, full equality of the races and full freedom for blacks. This impetus came from a coalescence of Federal power, Northern missionary zeal and black initiative. Inevitably, the thrust of these forces evoked hostility and opposition from much of the white South.

Meantime, north of the Mason-Dixon line, there had also been efforts to promote the education of blacks. A few persons braved local obloquy and physical harm in order to educate black children in New England. And two religious denominations (one white, one black) founded two colleges for blacks even before the Civil War—in Pennsylvania and Ohio.

All these efforts to provide higher education for blacks addressed the task by supplying separate institutions. Some of them, to be sure, were chartered with broader language, even though circumstances prevented them from having more than token white enrollments. Two notable exceptions to this general practice were Oberlin College, founded in Ohio in 1833 for "the coeducation of the sexes and the races," and Berea College in Kentucky (1855) with the same objective.

With the disbanding of the Freedmen's Bureau and the reversing of trends it had advocated, the 1880's and 1890's saw state after state in the South establishing public colleges for Negroes. Ultimately, seventeen of these separate state institutions were created. The segregating states wanted to participate in the program of Land Grant Universities; but they could do so under the law only if there were institutions within their own borders which, using the Federal grants, admitted Negroes. The separate-but-equal formula which was later to be enshrined in the *Plessy v. Ferguson* decision was thus institutionalized in the seventeen State Colleges for Negroes. Separate they were; but they were "equal" (in the sense that Federal funds were fairly apportioned on the basis of racial population ratios) in Oklahoma only. And none of the seventeen, before 1954, reflected an effective public concern for equal quality of higher education within the framework of separation.

Thus, the genesis of the public-controlled college for Negroes was markedly different from that of the private colleges, and their year-to-year existence was a triumph of frugality and compromise under paternalistic state control. Nevertheless, the record of these state colleges in service to the nation and particularly to black citizenry is an enviable one. The situation varies from state to state; but with the possible exception of West Virginia, it can be asserted that none of the former segregating states has yet begun to provide for its black citizens, in institutions founded for blacks, an educational opportunity which approaches in quality and stature that which is provided for students at its institutions founded for whites. It would appear to be unspoken policy to make sure that whatever integration takes place under compulsion of court decision and Federal order will take place in such a way as to bring greater strength to the institutions founded for whites.

There are now in existence 111 colleges and universities which were founded for Negroes. Two of these in West Virginia, and one in Missouri now belong properly in a new category: "*Formerly* predominantly Negro." The two in West Virginia are nearly three-fourths white in their undergraduate enrollment. At Jefferson City, Missouri, Lincoln University is just over fifty per cent white in its undergraduate enrollment.

Enrollment data by race are available for the undergraduates in eighty-eight of the colleges which were founded for Negroes and which, because of their having programs which are federally funded, must supply enrollment data by race.[1] These data show, for the most recent year available (Fall 1968) that the two institutions in West Virginia (Bluefield State and West Virginia State) enroll more than one-third of the total number of white students enrolled in all of the entire group of colleges founded for Negroes. Something more than another third are enrolled in institutions founded for Negroes in Ohio, Pennsylvania and Missouri. The remaining institutions founded for Negroes have scarcely reached the "token" level of integration: less than one student in two thousand is a Caucasian. Thirty-three show no white enrollment whatever.

It may therefore be concluded that even though racial equality and freedom may have been an important part of the origins and historical legacy of colleges and universities founded for Negroes, racial integration within their own student bodies is not at the present time an accomplished fact in 108 of the 111. In its Cincinnati Statement,[2] the National Board of Directors of the National Association for the Advancement of Colored People flatly asserts its belief that the time has come to make a concerted push for integration of the student bodies of the institutions founded for Negroes.

The reasons are many. In the chapter which follows, the debate is extended. At this point of the discussion, we note that if integration is to have any validity over the long haul, it must be a two-way street. All over the nation, blacks object when a particular integration program calls for busing of black children only, or for the abandonment of formerly all-black institutions only. Negroes have a legitimate complaint when integration means merely that blacks do all the integrating. The complaint is legitimate; but its legitimacy is open to question when the complainers make no effective effort to achieve racial integration at the colleges where they are themselves in full control. With thirty-three out of 111 institutions showing no white enrollment whatever, and with seventy-five of the remaining enrolling an average of less than one white per two-thousand enrollees, and when most of these white enrollees are merely exchange students resident for a semester or so on leave from a northern Alma Mater, the demand from the black campus that racial equality should prevail becomes strangely muted. All legal barriers to integration have been removed since 1954. Integration is legally possible on any campus anytime and anywhere in the United States of America; and since 1964, the weight of law has required "affirmative compliance" with the integration effort. Blacks have rightly objected when they were treated like pawns in the integration game. They have an opportunity to leave the wailing

---

[1] Undergraduate Enrollment by Ethnic Group in Federally Funded Institutions of Higher Education: Fall 1968. Office for Civil Rights, U. S. Dept. of H.E.W. Washington 1969.

[2] See Appendix.

22

and complaining to others, and to lead the way in establishing integration as a fact of national life. They have only to move aggressively and affirmatively to integrate the institutions over which they have policy control.

The white student will not come without some special attention—just as the black student failed to flock to northern institutions until very recent efforts were made to recruit and retain him. The white boy or girl is no better prepared, psychologically or through experience, for life at the black campus than is the black student for the typical white campus. Programs of recruitment, with appropriate support services, to bring white students to the formerly all-black campus must therefore be accompanied by a conscious ordering of curricula and extra-curricular matters to make sure that all students—not just the black—are served well. Teachers and administrators cannot assume that the black college is ready for the white enrollee without some additional institutional preparation, any more than their counterparts on the white campus can correctly assume that the white college is fully ready for black enrollees. In later chapters, we have more to say on this matter, but we point out at this stage that the desirable goal of integration will remain nothing but a goal unless there is serious and sustained effort to make all campuses multi-racial. It will do little good to open up the formerly all-white campuses to black enrollment without similarly opening the gates of the institutions founded for blacks.

There is an alternative. Its prototype is the tribal college established in South Africa as an instrument of apartheid. Just as the University of Witwatersrand has been forced to close its doors to Bantus, Coloureds and Indians; and just as Fort Hare has been forced to shut out its former white enrollees; so, all three of the "Bantu Colleges" and the two institutions for Indians and Coloureds, collectively serve the purposes of apartheid: white supremacy through separation.

Of course, the college in the United States which was founded for Negroes would, in the short run, have a much easier time of it if it continued to be for one race only. It would have the applause, if not the active support, of all the forces of segregation. This is a clearly proven fact. Three former governors in southern states last year gave unqualified support to the proposal by Roy Innis, currently head of C.O.R.E., that segregated schools and colleges should be the accepted order of the day in their states, with each race running its own schools and colleges for its own people only. It remains to be proved, however, that the easiest way is always the best or that it is right. The effort to make former Negro colleges into bi-racial and multi-racial institutions should not be abandoned without a try.

The multi-racial faculty is already an established fact at a majority of the colleges founded for blacks. There is no sound reason why any faculty should be exclusively of a single race: all the reasons for such restriction are unsound. They will not stand the critical light of open discussion. To be sure, there can be no assumption that every white person under consideration for appointment to the faculty of a college founded for Negroes is automatically acceptable simply because he is acceptable at a white institution. Persons with racial bias will do enough damage on a campus which is restricted to mainly persons of their own color. Despite conscientious recruitment and screening, there will doubtless continue to be occasions when the pink slip appears in the pay envelope, especially for that most vicious of all racists, the paternalist. The point applies with equal force, in reverse, on the campus of the white institution. Indeed, it is difficult to understand or accept the argument that an individual is qualified to teach in any institution—white or black or integrated—if he is not color blind.

Meanwhile, in those few institutions founded for blacks and in which large proportions of white students have now enrolled, the nation will watch with considerable interest to make sure that the results of transition are acceptable. Will white presidents replace black at Jefferson City, Missouri, and at Bluefield and Charleston, West Virginia? Will the faculties now become increasingly white only? Will programs for the benefit of ethnic minorities cease to have vitality and viability? Or will a genuine integration take place and be perpetuated, establishing institutions which are in fact color-blind? Only the people and the governments of Missouri and West Virginia have the power to answer these questions; but much depends on the answers given.

This chapter, up to this point, has been concerned very largely with the question of integration on the campus of the institutions founded for Negroes. As we move on to other aspects of the subject, let it be remarked that the publicly-controlled institutions for blacks are just as much under obligation to conform to the law, the courts and the Constitution as are the publicly-controlled institutions founded for whites. The fact that the black colleges have not yet been haled into court for violation of the 14th Amendment does not relieve them of their obligation. They are merely temporary beneficiaries of benign neglect on the part of those who are charged with the responsibility of enforcing the law without reference to race or color. As for the private institutions, if they have federally-funded programs, they stand to lose that funding whenever a showing is made that they fail to enroll students without reference to race. Finally, if it be argued that whites will not enroll in formerly all-black institutions, the answer is that they do enroll when given favorable opportunity. West Virginia and Missouri prove that fact.

But whether they integrate their student bodies swiftly or cautiously, the colleges founded for Negroes have additional jobs to do. They have a very special job to do in enabling the black student to "get it

24

all together," to be what he innately is—equal. They already know well the difference between equal opportunity and opportunity to be equal. It remains to act on that knowledge.

Over the short run, the colleges founded for blacks can supply to the rest of the nation's colleges and universities a stream of men and women who know well the meaning of the Black Experience and who are equipped to step into graduate schools and to go on into the faculties of the formerly white institutions. These will be students of both races. Only a few of them will be going into the teaching of Black Studies on the formerly all-white campus. Over the short run these colleges founded for Negroes must continue to discharge the functions which history has placed almost exclusively on their shoulders: the educating of thousands of black youth in an ethos of ethnic self-discovery and self-respect. They will of necessity continue to supply the remedial opportunities which correct the inadequacies of elementary and secondary schooling of the ghetto and of the rural countryside. They will do these things without being unduly bemused by the breast-beating of tardy northern institutions which currently proclaim their self-satisfaction in having at long last started appropriate remedial programs for ghettoized urban slum dwellers.

Over the long haul, the college founded for Negroes will find its fulfillment in working itself out of a job as a segregated institution. It will begin to take seriously the full meaning of the words of the Supreme Court in *Brown v. Board of Education:*

"Does segregation of children in public schools solely on the basis of race, even though the physical facilities and other 'tangible' factors may be equal, deprive the children of the minority group of equal educational opportunities? We believe that it does."

The self segregating college is still segregated.

The decade of the Sixties was ushered in by four black students who, in Greensboro, North Carolina, decided that they would sit down at a lunch counter and stay there until they were served. The decade ended with guns at Jackson State College. Bracketed by these incidents, the 1960s were characterized by an increasing tempo of student activism in matters of racial concern. On not a few campuses of colleges founded for Negroes, this student activism brought a degree of institutional turmoil and unrest. In a few instances that trouble was as disruptive as was the spreading Berkeley syndrome at northern universities. Most of the matters which troubled the campuses of the colleges founded for whites have also been matters of concern on the black campuses. Most of the remarks about campus troubles and the remedies for them in this little book apply more or less equally to both the black and the white student and to both the black and the white college. There is one particular in which the college founded for Negroes is precisely similar to the college founded for whites, namely: If the students don't see the president and faculty actively engaged in wrestling with the evils of racism, they will (a) demand that a show of action be made, (b) disrupt or disturb or otherwise inconvenience the institution when response to that demand is slow or grudging or inadequate, and (c) give the institution a degree of campus calm only when surcease has been earned by performance.

That the disturbance of the Sixties were less pervasive and less violent on the average campus for blacks than on the white counterpart campus is due, in part, to the traditional restraints which racial caste has forced upon the black man, despite the upsurging of internal rage. It is also due, in part, to the fact that at least some of the presidents of colleges founded for Negroes were arrested along with their students and faculty members on the picket lines and in the sit-ins. They earned their spurs in jail and in the defendants' box along with their students. It is incidental that the cause in which students, teachers and administrators thus acted together was the battle for racial justice and freedom and ethnic identity and dignity. That fact does not detract from the common-sense heroism of the participating administrators, even though it explains the readiness of their participation.

If the colleges founded for Negroes have known a little less turmoil in the 1960's than their white counterparts, it might be a matter of wisdom for them not to press their luck unduly. While white radicals have run through a succession of consecutive issues, from Free Speech to Ecology; and while Black Recognition has been a constantly recurring issue on a majority of the campuses despite this ambivalence; it remains true that among black students the question of race has been the dominant issue, sometimes the only issue. And that issue promises to be around for a while.

At the conclusion of the preceding chapter, stress was laid on the necessity for creating a new spirit and of expressing that spirit in action. These words are not repeated in connection with the college founded for Negroes—not because these truths do not apply here with equal force, but because most black readers already know these facts, whether they admit it or not. Repetition would therefore be insultingly redundant, except for those few persons whose bitter life-experience has so blinded them that nothing short of tearing off their eyelids would make them see the truth.

Coolness, hostility and contempt will not lure white students to the formerly all-black campus; and if blacks persist in holding themselves aloof, they will invite and enforce apartheid and continue to be, institutionally, denied their fair share of public and private funds.

The spirit, expressed through action, finally determines results.

26

CHAPTER V

THE CENTRAL ISSUE

It took the courts eighty-six years and the Congress ninety-six to recognize that the 13th, 14th and 15th Amendments had made the Constitution color-blind. During all this time, and continuing through the present and into the future, there has been sharp debate and continuing division of opinion as to what politico-socio-economic goals were to be preferred.

Stated goals have ranged along a spectrum somewhat as follows:

1. *Extinction.* Under Hitler's leadership and war-time hysteria, Nazi Germany killed six million Jews and millions more who sympathized with them. Genocide remains as one of the positions advocated for "solving the race question."

2. *Expulsion.* The American Colonization Society, from its founding in 1817, advocated that all persons of Negro ancestry should be resettled in Africa.

3. *Back to Mother Africa.* Led by Marcus Garvey in the 1920s, the Universal Negro Improvement Association advocated emigration (not expulsion) by persons of Negro ancestry, in preference to second-class citizenship in America.

4. *Segregation.* Separation of the races by law, as national policy, is the desire of those who advocate White Supremacy. In South Africa, segregation is called "Apartheid" (rhymes with "hate"). Many in the United States support segregation as a desirable goal.

5. *Separatism.* Sometimes called "voluntary segregation," separatism accepts ethnic separatism as the basis for ethnic strength and empowerment.

6. *Black Nationalism.* Either in the return to Africa, or in a piece of the United States carved out by a self-determining Black Nation with blacks in control just as whites are in the rest of the country. First seriously proposed by the American Communist Party, this alternative has had support at various times by some Black Nationalist groups.

7. *Amalgamation.* Seldom advocated by anyone as national policy, but not infrequently used by opponents of equality of the races as a diversionary device, the biological fusion of the races has no possibility of becoming a compulsory feature of American law. Instead, there is continuous voluntary intermixture, both within and outside of the marriage bond.

8. *Integration.* The integrated society would be one in which ancestry was neither an advantage nor a disability to any person or group. Affirmative valuation would be placed on diversity and freedom to be different-or-alike-in-equality-and-mutual-respect. Such a color-blind society is clearly prescribed by the Constitution. Progress toward that goal has been neither swift nor continuous.

In the early nineteenth century, the controversy over these issues was triangular: slavery versus colonization versus abolition. The abolitionists, led by William Lloyd Garrison and strongly supported by such Negro activists as Frederick Douglass, Sojourner Truth and Charlotte Forten, were effective in defeating the colonization effort by mid-century—at least at the propaganda level. But the argument between the abolitionists and the pro-slavery forces persisted right through the Civil War. It continues today in the form of integration versus segregation.

The last quarter of the nineteenth century witnessed the resurgence of White Supremacy, the post-Reconstruction period. Black men walked a "perilous terrain" if they tried to assume positions of leadership in the South. It was at the Atlanta Exposition in 1895 that Booker T. Washington proposed his famous compromise: "In all things essential to common welfare, as one as the hand, yet in all things social separate as the fingers." And a decade later, W. E. B. DuBois brought together twenty-nine Negro intellectuals and professional men to found the "Niagara Movement" which was designated to repudiate the Atlanta compromise of Booker T. Washington and to lay the basis for the twentieth century fight for freedom. They demanded access to the ballot, an end to discrimination in public accommodations, equal education, and the enforcement of the Constitution. Four years later, in 1909, the Niagara Movement merged into a larger interracial effort which was called the National Association for the Advancement of Colored People and which aimed at attaining equality, eradicating caste and race prejudice, securing justice in the courts and complete equality before the law, together with equal opportunity in education, housing and employment. By 1950, the NAACP had come to demand the complete elimination of segregation as such. That effort continues.

But not every black man or woman appears to support the goals championed by the NAACP. (It goes without saying that there are whites who do not share these goals.) In this country, the first notable opposition by blacks to integration-and-equality came from the Universal Negro Improvement Association which the colorful and flamboyant Marcus Garvey founded and led. Himself a West Indian, Garvey did not believe that equality would be conceded by the white man in America: he therefore advocated a return to Africa, to prove that Negroes were capable of establishing a superior civilization.

Garvey lifted the adjective "black" to a new level of dignity and pride, even though he called his organization, the "Universal *Negro* Improvement Association." He preached black solidarity, declaring that God and Christ were black. He called on all black men and women to reject white standards and to create their own. UNIA developed into a mass movement, with chapters in many cities. Parades and demonstrations helped to raise funds for the purchase of a ship ("Black Star Line") intended to ferry Negroes "back to Africa." The Black Star line foundered; Garvey went to prison; the movement died even before he did—in 1940, penniless and with his dreams shattered. But one thing Garvey accomplished: he left a permanent legacy of pride in blackness, a legacy which enriches the present day.

Black nationalism had little support in the United States after Garvey's venture failed, until the Black Muslim movement emerged in 1930, headed by W. Fard of Detroit who recruited a Sandersville, Georgia, Negro named Elijah Poole. Poole became Elijah Muhammad, succeeded Fard in 1934 and moved the organization's headquarters to Chicago. Claiming more than 250,000 followers, the movement is essentially religious; but because of their activities, the Muslims are also considered to be a protest movement. They eschew cooperation with whites, demand an end to police brutality and exemption from taxation as long as Negroes are deprived of equal justice, desire complete separation in their own state or territory, prohibit intermarriage. They have established schools and businesses, grocery stores, restaurants and bakery and farming enterprises. They publish a weekly newspaper, *Muhammad Speaks*, which reports the world news of black men and women.

The most prominent disciple of Elijah Muhammad was Malcolm X who was brutally murdered in 1965, two years after leaving the Muslims and founding his own organization, the Organization for Afro-American Unity. His departure from the Muslims was not voluntary: he had commented on the assassination of President John Kennedy by saying something about "chickens coming home to roost," and Elijah Muhammad immediately suspended him. During his brief leadership, the OAAU made little headway: but since his death, Malcolm X has been elevated to a level of adulation amounting almost to deification. Youthful writers and black chauvinists, supported by sectors of the news media, have been particularly assiduous in promoting the memory of Malcolm X and perpetuating his philosophy.

During his lifetime, Malcolm X asserted the right of self-defense, maximum retaliation against white racists, and pride in blackness on the part of "so-called Negroes." He derided the "white man's Christian world," called white people "devils," and spoke of black people in America as having been "colonized, enslaved, lynched, exploited, deceived, abused and degraded." He urged black unity, peace and the use of guns and knives—but only against non-blacks. He urged blacks

29

to cease harming one another, and to quit harming themselves through the use of whiskey, dope, reefers and cigarettes. He condemned gambling and urged thrift, demanded the end of fornication and adultery and prostitution, opposed interracial dating or marriage, urged respect for black womanhood and an end to all immoral practices. He eschewed political parties—except those which might support the black man's aspirations, as he interpreted them.

The Malcolm X philosophy urged an all-out war on organized crime, the exposure of bribe-taking policemen in black communities, the establishing of clinics to aid drug addicts and unwed mothers, a guardian system to help black youth in trouble, charity within the black community, aid to black veterans, and pride in working together to regain "our self-respect, manhood, dignity and freedom," in closer association with the African past.

But the field was not to be left exclusively to Elijah Muhammad and Malcolm X (with one of their better-known recruits, Muhammad Ali, the former Cassius Clay). In 1966, two young disenchanted black activists, Huey P. Newton and Bobby Seale founded the Black Panther Party for Self-Defense, in Oakland, California. Although the black panther had for years been the symbol of the Prairie View A & M College in Texas, it is probable that Newton and Seale selected the name because of the example of the Lowndes County "Freedom Organization in Alabama" which under SNCC in 1965 conducted voter registration campaigns, and which used the black panther as its emblem.

Working closely with SNCC in the beginning, the Panthers designated SNNC leader H. "Rap" Brown Honorary Minister of Justice, Stokely Carmichael, Honorary Prime Minister, James Foreman, Honorary Minister of Foreign Affairs.

In May, 1967, members of the Panthers invaded the State Assembly chamber in Sacramento with guns in hand in what appears to have been a publicity stunt. A lot of important people were scared that day.

The inflammatory rhetoric of this group has appealed to many youth, although disenchantment is observed as schisms and internal violence have developed. Panthers are credited with popularizing the terms "pigs" for police, "off the pigs" for kill, "honky" or "Whitey" for white and "right on." They have been pictured all over America armed with daggers or guns, with bodyguards standing with folded arms or clenched fists, uniformed in black leather jackets, cartridge belt and berets worn on top of Afro-styled hair, a bullet suspended around the neck.

The leading spokesman of the Panthers is Eldridge Cleaver, author of *Soul On Ice* (1967) and *Eldridge Cleaver* (1969). After his release from San Quentin prison, Cleaver served as Minister of Information of the Party. Now in self-exile in Algeria, Cleaver has had a tremendous impact on young blacks as well as many white youths.

In his writings Cleaver debunked the ethnic standards of whites, insisted on the use of "black" in an uplifted sense, denigrated integration as a goal for blacks, urged pride in Afro-Americanism and the use of the term "black power," called on Negroes to stop killing other Negroes and to start killing police, urged resistance to white authority. Cleaver maneuvered the Panthers into coalition with the Peace and Freedom Party, an anti-war group.

The Black Panthers have been engaged in a number of gun battles with the police resulting in the death of several of their number.

The dogmatism of the Panther Party caused Carmichael to quit, in July, 1969, condemning its alliances with white radicals.

The well-publicized (and now largely abandoned) Panther breakfast program may be seen as a Marxist scheme to indoctrinate ghetto youngsters into revolutionary ideology and extremist anti-white hatred, to operate as a cloak for illegal activities, such as shakedowns, rackets and vice.

The romanticism of the Panthers has undoubtedly appealed to some black college students who may not agree with the aims of the group but affect their rhetoric and style of dress, and often adopt many of their mannerisms.

Among the many factors which contribute to campus ferment and unrest, the new separatism which is here under review must be rated as being of considerable importance. Certainly it must be taken into account and dealt with honestly and openly.

Racial separatism has no place in the United States. The back eddies of the centuries continue to carry the chips of chance in their little circles; but the mainstream sweeps on toward the broad ocean and those who ride that mainstream scarcely know that the backwaters exist. The choice before the United States of America as a nation is whether or not to welcome black Americans into the mainstream; and the choice which black Americans can make (no one else can make it for them) is whether or not to leave the backwater and ride the open currents. Both these queries should be given affirmative answers. The new separatism is an asset insofar as it emphasizes self-awareness and self-respect and self-help and self-confidence and self-pride in blackness; but it is a liability insofar as it denigrates other races or counsels that blacks should "go it alone." Blacks must be ready for the journey in the mainstream of America, and American campuses must help to make sure both that the blacks are ready and that the rest of the nation also is prepared for the merging of forces.

Of the eight general possibilities with which this chapter began, there is promise for the future of black America and of the whole of America only in the eighth, Integration—the Open Society.

CHAPTER VI

THE CURRICULUM

In recent times, particularly since the murder of Dr. Martin Luther King, Jr., many colleges and universities, with newly acquired social sensitivity, have been agonizing over the question of which black students might become qualified to be on campus—and how to qualify them. Remedial programs to correct academic inadequacies have blossomed, financial support and counselling services have been provided, and special consideration or status for the "disadvantaged" or the "culturally deprived" have been devised. Helpful as these innovations may have been, and necessary as they may continue to be, in increasing and retaining black enrollment, they are not the answer because they respond to the wrong question.

Instead of asking only: How may selected black students be qualified to be on campus? Colleges and universities should also be asking: How may campuses become qualified to serve the needs of black students? This question needs to be asked on all campuses—both the so-called predominantly white and the so-called predominately black.

As instruments for transmitting the social and cultural heritage to each on-coming generation, the American college has emphasized Western culture and civilization, that is, western Europe and North America. Stimulated by two world wars and reflecting an internationalism which some have lately castigated as veiled imperialism, the American college has added Area Studies to provide special kinds of information and expertise about selected parts of the world other than Western Europe and the United States. Russian Studies have flourished and Chinese Studies have been promoted—sometimes because of special political issues and interests. The scholars produced in programs of Area Studies have been of considerable service to various foreign programs of the United States and to international programs of the United Nations. They have also populated the proliferating Centers of Area Studies. But, by and large, the mainstream of meaning in higher education in the United States has flowed from ancient Greece and Rome through medieval and modern Europe, across the Atlantic, to fill the reservoirs of learning within a western-oriented parochial America. As for the strictly American cultural component, it is typified by the fact that "American Literature" included James Fennimore Cooper but not James Weldon Johnson. Since the roots and branches of American civilization are thought to be strictly "Western," the African in-put to American culture has been ignored. Thus, the culture transmitted to each on-coming generation is essentially that of Western Europe with a gloss of white America.

Secondly, as instruments for the maturing and self-discovery of young adults, the American college and university have held out the hope that students would become educated ladies and gentlemen. That is to say, the dominant purpose has been to produce persons of intelligence and compassion who would subscribe to and perpetuate the standards and values of the American white middle class. Again, this was not the work of knaves or fools: it was the high-minded effort of stalwart citizens to bring up the next generation in its own image. More accurately, its self-image.

Thirdly, as centers for training in the professions, in science and the social sciences, and in the arts, although some campuses have made gestures in other directions or instituted innovations of some significance, it is fair to say that the white campuses have generally expected all students to be educated for entrance into a white American society and successful performance therein. Many exceptions to this rule have been well-intentioned but paternalistic efforts to equip black students who enrolled at white institutions to be useful in later life in "serving their own people." Still other campuses have never stopped to examine their uncritically held belief that the American Dream would automatically fulfill itself if only more and more persons were educated in the genteel ideals of a democratic society.

Following on the inner-city explosions of the 1960s and, particularly, after the death of Martin Luther King, Jr., "Black Studies" emerged on the all-white campus as a means of dealing with the newly arriving and aggressive black student. In some instances, such programs had already been in preparation or in being. In most, however, they were improvised to meet militant demands with instant curricula. These demands were something more than slogans and something less than programs. The response to them was about the same.

What, then, must the formerly all-white campus do to make itself fit for the black student? It must ask that question of itself, and keep asking it, never expecting a complete and final answer but always expecting new and better questions to emerge with continuous questing and adaption.

Curriculum at the Negro Colleges

All but a handful of the predominantly Negro colleges are located in the former segregating states. By law and by custom, enrollment has been and continues to be predominantly—almost exclusively—uni-racial. And within these all-black institutions, the underlying assumptions of American higher education in general have been accepted. Just as in the formerly all-white institutions, so in the black colleges, the aims are: to acquaint the student with the mainstream of western civilization, to afford opportunity for self-discovery and maturity in terms of middle class values, and to insure the professional competence to "make it" in a white man's world. Not a few of the more than one hundred black institutions have also attempted to build within the student a self-image of dignity and of pride in his blackness, and their graduates have known that black was beautiful long before the slogan was coined. Yet few of the black institutions have been completely emancipated from the heavy burden of history dating from slavery and post-Reconstruction. The terms on which white America suffered the black institutions to exist did not include the rejection of racial caste. So it has come about that in the all-black institution, the curricula of the white prototype have been duplicated— plus, in some notable instances, special concerns not dissimilar to the Area Studies of white institutions but directed toward Africa and peoples of African descent in the Caribbean and in the United States.

Nor have the black institutions effectively avoided the errors of white colleges in the rush to produce instant "Black Studies." In all too many instances, it has been a scissors-and-paste job which brought together in the catalog existing courses which dealt with Negro aspects of American life, changed the label from "Negro" to "Black," and taught the same old courses in the same old way.

It is too soon to evaluate the impact of The Institute of the Black World in the reshaping of academic objectives and the creating of new curricula. If the temptations of separatism are successfully resisted, it may prove to be a seminal influence on Academe.

The predominantly black institution, much like its white counterpart, must also ask itself what it must do to be fit for black students and for the whites whom it must increasingly enroll if integration is to be a two-way street. It must ask these questions and keep on asking them, refusing easy answers or miracle cures wrapped in slogans.

Concerns Common to Both White and Black Colleges

It is imperative that the white student, every white student, learn about and affirmatively accept his entire heritage as an American. The parochial blinders must come off. All the historical facts and personages and movements woven into the fabric of American life must be included in American history. The white student, at least as much as the black, has need to understand and to accept the contributions of black America as data of his own existence. No single American history textbook now in print supplies this need. The white student needs also to find the data of the social sciences dealing with black social phenomena in some category other than the pathological. It is only partly true to say that the white student needs black studies more than does the black: the full truth is that he needs to have the whole picture in all its completeness before him if he is to understand even that portion which his white-oriented college has traditionally given him.

34

It is equally important that no black student be denied access to *his* full cultural heritage. As an American, he has just as much right to benefit from and take pride in the contributions of his fellows of all colors as does anyone else. And long after the artificial self-consciousness of recently discovered pride in blackness has ripened into a secure self-respect which has no need for rhetorical superlatives because it is secure, the black student will still need to know well what riches have been brought to American culture and American life by black men and women and their descendants through the centuries.

There is an alternative to the foregoing assertions. It is segregation, separatism: the building of two societies, increasingly separate and determinedly hostile. It is the pattern established in southern Africa and in process of being established in Rhodesia. The tribal colleges for blacks lay heavy emphasis on tribal identity and tribal pride; but they are tools of white domination just as surely as are the universities reserved for whites. Separate curricula, even though they enhance the self-image of each respective group, are tools of separatism, barriers in the path toward one society.

In short, no curriculum is good enough either for a white student or for a black student unless it is good for both.

CHAPTER VII

THE EXTRA-CURRICULAR

Sometimes extra-curricular matters are referred to as "activities," implying that in matters of the curriculum, the student is to be passive. But on campuses where curricular matters have become areas of active learning rather than of passively being taught, it is all the more important that the learning values in extra-curricular life be given overt attention. Not as a substitute for an inclusive curriculum which honors the values and meets the needs of minorities as well as majorities, but as the extra-curricular complement of an adequate curriculum, the extra-curricular arenas call for scrutiny and aggressive action.

Two overriding concerns should direct and stimulate all extra-curricular areas of the campus and its community: (1) to make sure that access to and participation in all extra-curricular matters is free and open to all and (2) to make sure that the variety and character of the extra-curricular is rich enough and flexible enough to enlist not only the majority group member but also the minority, and to be rewarding when participated in.

Partial participation and parochialism are not enough: merely to be exposed to the prevailing culture and values which, on the typical American campus are those of the middle class, is not an adequate experience for the black student on the white campus. Neither is it adequate for the white student, whether on the white campus or the black. And the black student on the black campus also needs a wider exposure than that which comes solely through the perpetuation of the life-style and values of his home community. The extra-curricular affairs of the campus can become the means of creating the attitudes and learning the values of the cosmopolitan man, one who, with Euripides, can say,

"The whole expanse of air is open to the eagle's flight, and every land is native soil to the noble man."

This does not mean disparaging the life-style and values of any group, however parochial. It does not mean denigrating one culture in order to admire another. On the contrary, it means knowing one's own native culture well and being proudly conscious of it, while at the same time having broad and inclusive empathy for what others admire or hold dear. It is tolerance, but it is much more: it is affirmative affection for difference, a high disregard for externals which separate and a high regard for commonalities which unite—while at the same time holding to an unashamed and unabashed pride in one's self and one's own group identity. Where custom and history have rated the values of a minority lower than those of the majority, such a goal calls for corrective revision of the patterns of campus life as a means of correcting the larger society. Where tradition and usage have tended to make the minority hypersensitive and defensive in relation to its own history and present status, such a goal calls for corrective action which makes aggressive defensiveness unnecessary. In short, the Open Society does not welcome inequalities based on choice of ancestors: The Open Society is open. It encourages each individual to be his own best self, as a member both of the larger society and of his own smaller segment. It does not homogenize the culture: it respects and maintains variety. It does not demand conformity where creativity can be encouraged.

Now, the black student who enrolls on the typical white campus has his own special kinds of problems in achieving these goals. Usually, he will come from a home-and-community experience in which he has been protected, to some degree, from the seeming coldness and indifference of a white American culture. Quite commonly, he will also have had at least some preliminary warnings of the loneliness that comes to the black boy or girl who suddenly finds himself away from home in a strange world; he may even have had some experience in patterns of rejection, revolt and violence as cultures clashed. There is one role, however, which the black student is tired of playing: he no longer wants his peers who are white to treat him as though he were some sort of Exhibit A for their tolerance. He wants a chance to be himself, without always knowing that he will be confronted in chance conversation by the well-meaning white student who wants to know "How does it feel to be black?" In short, the black student wants to be able to be himself, without embarrassment and without extra demands on him because of his blackness—no matter whether these extra demands come from those who do not like him and do not want him around, or whether they come from those who want to show that they like him but do not know how to let him feel at home.

Under these circumstances, with the sudden growth of black enrollments on the formerly all-white campuses, pressures have recently been exerted in the direction of neo-separatism. In order to be able to relax and to be himself, the black student has requested a chance to live together with others of his own group; and when the request has been denied, he has demanded it, sometimes with a show of force. Well-meaning white administrators have, in some instances, granted these demands, setting up all-black residential quarters and eating facilities. Soul food and soul music and the Afro life-style have, in these instances, been a means of reenforcing group identity and challenging the dominance of the prevalent culture. The black experience has also been used as a retreat from the uncertainties and ambivalence of the dominant culture.

Experience has shown, however, that merely to grant the black students' request for separation is to fail and to fail them as well. It does not secure campus peace and calm (a value which falsely motivated some administrative actions in this area). It does not give either the black or the white student a full opportunity to grow and develop either as an individual or as a member of the group into which he was born. This ready resort to neo-separatism fails because it does not go beneath the surface demands, to get at the root of the difficulties.

The most common reasons given for neo-separatist demands are: "Tired of being an experimental guinea pig for white students," "Lack of commonality with white students, thus no basis for meaningful conversation or contact," "All whites are phony and devoid of an understanding or appreciation of black culture and physiological differences," and "Soul food is not served in the cafeteria." But these are not reasons: they are excuses.

Surely it must be realized that racial grouping based exclusively on skin color does not offer a cure-all for racial discontent. Separation, indeed, leads only to greater separateness and alienation. The ignorance of both blacks and whites about each other is increased by separation. Colleges are alleged to be established for the purpose of combatting and correcting ignorance—not encouraging it.

The general point of view we have been stating is not automatically translated into specifics. It requires a high degree of concern, understanding and intelligence, together with an absolute refusal to condescend. It requires specific decision and action, leading to the establishing of congenial patterns of the extra-curricular in campus life.

In housing, it is quite usual to permit upperclassmen to select roommates. We see nothing wrong with this, and do not question the choices which may result. What we do challenge is the notion that an entire building, or section or wing or floor of a building should be set aside for whites only—or for blacks only.

The dining hall or cafeteria menu should reflect the diversity that exists among the student body. On occasion, special foods associated with special groups should be featured—and served to all. No student should go through month after month of institutional food without finding an occasional moment in which he gets something like what he got "back home." If these qualities of cuisine are beyond the imagination of the director of food services, then the director should be reeducated or fired.

The visiting entertainment and cultural groups and personalities which are brought to campus or to nearby theatres and concert halls should include members of minority and majority groups. Entertainers, artists, consultants, lecturers, etc., can be a rich resource for a fuller experience.

More importantly, the theatre and performing arts on campus need to be made inclusive and kept in lively variety. The traditional activities on the formerly white campus have been formed by white students to meet their recreational and cultural needs. To open these campus organizations and activities to wider participation is necessary; and to afford to black students an equal opportunity freely to express their own primary interests and values as a normally expected campus occurrence is equally necessary. Thespian groups have ignored a valuable wealth of drama based on black experience. Musical organizations reveal ignorance of jazz. Both reflect the absence of black faculty who might serve as sponsors for new activities or contribute meaningfully to existing programs. On the black campus, the problem is sometimes the precise reverse of the situation on the white campus.

Sports have traditionally been praised as the great opportunity to demonstrate the equality of the races; but intercollegiate sports as practiced on the American campus have left much to be desired. When three black athletes raised their clenched fists in salute as they received their Olympic medals in Mexico City, they were not reflecting personal pique. They were demonstrating a deeply felt need, a need which is felt throughout the whole sports world, a need for recognition without having to overcome racial barriers. Universities and colleges which have built their intercollegiate records on the strength of black athletes (recruited for the purpose) have not always been quick to employ blacks in the coaching staff and have sometimes been accused of exploiting the black athlete for institutional aggrandizement. Heavy emphasis on intercollegiate sports has also sometimes led to undervaluation of intramural sports, which in turn has meant that the run of the mill student (black or white) has benefited less than he ought from athletics and that intercollegiate games have become merely a spectator sport. Under these circumstances, the status of athletes is much like that of gladiators in Roman arenas—and today's gladiators do not and will not recognize the right of a college president to settle a player's destiny with a jerk of the thumb, as though he were a Roman Emperor. There are specifics, many of them; but what is principally at stake is a feeling tone: it is a matter of self respect which expects respect from others and will not settle for less.

Before we leave the extracurricular, at least one more subject must be mentioned: opportunity for religious expression. Of all the culture patterns in American society, few are more distinctively differentiated as between the racial groups than are the religious denominations. The First Amendment to the Constitution prevents the establishment of any religion: it also proscribes any limitations on the free exercise thereof. And the varieties of religious experience are sufficiently great so that no single institutional offering of religious services and activities can possibly serve the needs of an entire student body. Where there are churches and temples in the immediate community which meet the several needs of all students, the campus may encourage attendance at these local institutions. Where these institutions of religion are not easily accessible, organized busing service can be provided; and where neither of the foregoing can meet the needs of all students, the campus can assume the obligation of encouraging at least occasional visits by clergy from outside the immediate community. While the availability of a congenial religious community will not be an entire answer to the problems of a lonely student, no college which is insensitive to the varieties of religious need ought to expect or to enjoy campus calm.

Black students on a white campus commonly identify with the status of the black community as a whole. There were times when this was not true—when the black student was ashamed of, or tried to forget, his ghetto or farm origins. Not so today. The black student finds himself more readily in the black community off campus than in the white community on campus. He is no longer ashamed or apologetic. And he is frequently lonely. Hence, the extracurricular life of the campus becomes of great importance to the black student, and to the extent that the black community near the campus can be brought within the active circle of institutional concern, to participate in the making of the quality of campus life and to benefit from the services of the college—to that extent, both the college and the community will be serving their own self-interest in meeting the needs of students.

There is one point at which extra-curricular activities of black students is unfortunately intensive. Over the recent years, they have been forced by a heightened consciousness of their needs and a slow-paced institutional response to those needs, to spend inordinate hours and energy in discussing and organizing and agitating for institutional change. They have, on occasion, dedicated entire blocks of several weeks or more solely to organized effort, protest, disruption. As students, both black and white, became increasingly adamant in their demands, and spent more and more of their energies attacking the institution and its administration, faculty and students, they had less time not only for their curricular studies but also for an enriched extra-curricular experience. The result has been seen not only in campus unrest but in gross miseducation. All that the students have learned from such experience is how to rebel and to conduct guerilla warfare. Is this the proper goal of college and university?

CHAPTER VIII

CAMPUS GOVERNANCE

The whole of collegiate life, not just the classroom and the laboratory and the library, should be designed to serve educational purposes. This is especially true of campus governance.

Whether we like it or not, educational administration does have an educational effect. An authoritarian campus, where president and deans stand *in loco parentis* (in place of parents) was the standard model in America down to World War II. Student restlessness ended that. The courts in 1866 had established the position of college administrators as stand-ins for parents, with full rights to discipline children (students) without limitations of due process. The courts reversed that status in 1961; but the spirit of *patria potestates* ("papa has the power") dies slowly, even when it is confronted with the spirit of *sui juris* ("I am my own law") in many a campus upheaval. The real lessons of college life are learned in the campus skirmishes and battles which these ancient phrases symbolize.

There are three levels of learning through campus experience: (1) the knowledge and information obtained from lectures, books, experiments, rap sessions with peer groups, and the like; (2) the skills and habits with which to manipulate and use this knowledge and information; and (3) the attitudes and values acquired incidentally but inevitably in the process of acquiring the first two. Thus, a student in class often learns how to be taught instead of learning how to learn. After graduation, he no longer learns because he has learned only how to be taught and he no longer has a teacher. Or again, a student may learn how to beat the game by studying the professor. Or—and this is the aspect which bears on the educative effect of campus governance—he learns either how to conform or how to rebel. Until very recent times, conformity or rebellion were the only real options open to the undergraduate, as the trustees insisted that the president sit *in loco parentis* and legislatures insisted that administrators exercise the full potential of *patres potestates*. The generation gap to one side, the major declaration of rebellious undergraduates from the Free Speech Movement to the Kent State and Jackson State tragedies, has been that if they have only the choice between conformity and rebellion, they choose to rebel.

If undergraduates are to learn how to be constructive instruments of social change, working through the processes of representative democracy, the campus must be structured to make that learning possible. They will not learn that lesson on a campus where the only alternatives are, "Do what the man says," or "Trash the place." On the other hand, no matter how efficient and effective the governance on a given campus may be in preserving the peace and avoiding disorder, the administrative process is miseducative in terms of educational goals unless it provides for the undergraduate a genuine experience in working as a member of a community which has the sense of controlling its own destiny because it continuously exercises the power to reshape campus life as it governs itself. It may be that the majority of American undergraduates have not yet come to the point of an open break with the social and political institutions of the nation and the men who sit in the seats of power; but undergraduates in large numbers have lost faith not only in American democracy but in the democratic process itself and in the utopias which beckoned former generations. They have lost this faith not because established patterns are evil but because they appear to be ineffective. They do not quickly correct injustice. They do not immediately respond to discrimination. They adjust too easily to uneasy compromise. And they afford no handle to be grasped by the undergraduate who wants to make things better.

Not least significant in the list of factors which lead to disillusionment with the processes of American campuses is the recent history of the civil rights struggle. Many persons, particularly those under twenty years of age, who were scarcely born when the Supreme Court rendered its verdict in the *Brown* case in 1954, mistook that decision as being the end of the struggle. It wasn't even the beginning of the end. It was only the end of the beginning. It merely put the full force of the courts and the Constitution on the side of racial justice, leaving the attainment of that goal to the people. Nevertheless, the idealism which poured out from the campus into the first sit-ins, the Freedom Rides and Freedom Marches and voter registration efforts, and the passing of Civil Rights legislation, represented the first great nation-wide opportunity for the American undergraduate, black or white, to have a genuine feeling of *sui juris*—of shaping destiny and striking an effective blow for a humane and democratic society of equals who hold each the other in mutual respect. As sixteen years of "all deliberate speed" left most black children still in segregated schools, as police dogs and water hoses and cattle prods in the streets were followed by the military presence on campus; as unions of construction workers stuck by their lily-white membership policies while black artisans walked the streets; as inner-city tenements were abandoned to the rats and junkies more rapidly than new housing was constructed; as the strident voices of extremists in both races escalated the vehemence of confrontation and exploited volatile emotions for venal purposes; and as a young generation which knew nothing of the

42

long struggle which had brought the nation to its moment of truth felt itself frustrated by a widening gap between the clear teachings and injunctions of the Constitution and the hopes of the American Dream on the one hand and on the other the lagging delay of social change, campus unrest came to sharp focus. Beleaguered college administrators were caught in the middle. Academic wheels turn exceedingly slow, and students were frustrated, impatient, angry. Thus, what students learned was, that regardless of reasons or excuses, results do not follow on any approach other than the violent confrontation, or at least the threat of such confrontation.

The point is that the processes and procedures of campus governance have not been such as to give either the black or the white student the feeling or the fact of active participation in rectifying the evils of racism. What the student has learned is that his choices are: (1) leave it alone or (2) tear it down. The student has not been afforded (3) the opportunity to build better. Bricks are therefore for throwing, not for building. Campus governance has been miseducative, more by inaction and the lethargy of inertia than by direct intent. Benign neglect has produced malignancy.

Not that there has been no effort to change campus governance. On the contrary, there are very few campuses on which major changes in campus governance have not brought new departures during the past decade. Most of these, as the surveys show, have reduced the powers of trustees and presidents while increasing the powers of faculties and (sometimes) of students. This trend has not corrected our difficulties: it has compounded them. As trustees and presidents have relinquished power, alumni and legislators and public officials and the public at large have demanded from these same authorities more stern handling of the campus, demanding authoritative postures from those who had just been stripped of authority and could only posture. Moreover, the newly-formed centers of power within the faculties or student bodies have not yet learned either the mode or the mood of making policies and deciding issues on the basis of justice, equity and social need.

Traditionally, it was only the president who, on campus, was charged with the responsibility to consider the interests of everyone. When he no longer exercises that function except through the weak processes of persuasive appeal, and when each newly emergent faculty or student group arrogates power hungrily while refusing to discipline itself for the common good, special interests come into control. If the former patterns of paternalism and authoritarianism miseducated the student, the newer patterns of group power exercised for narrow purpose are a poor substitute. What the student now learns from campus governance is that power comes to him who seizes it, and that he has the right to let that power corrupt him just as he believed others had been corrupted before him. The student learns not the lessons of democracy but of syndicalism or of anarchy or of guerrilla warfare.

If, then, campus governance is to contribute to the education, not the miseducation, of students, it must be so devised as to contribute to the education and re-education of faculty, administrators, trustees, public officials and legislators as well. Democracy will come not through seizure and counter-seizure of power, but through the sharing of power.

What should be done on a given campus? The particulars and specifics will vary a great deal. What is appropriate and necessary at a two-year community college will be inappropriate for a large residential university. Each institution, each campus, will best devise its own specifics.

But some general principles can be stated as useful guidelines: (1) The basic distinction between the making of policy and the executing of policy should be scrupulously observed. (2) Information on all matters of policy must be widely and easily available, with consciously devised processes for making sure that it is. (3) Overlapping jurisdictions must be avoided, while both discrete and common jurisdictions are clearly defined. (4) The processes of representation must be real enough to give each member of the campus community a genuine sense of participation, and open enough to assure his continual confidence. (5) The time lag must be compressed if the process of governance is to seem or to be real for the undergraduate whose months of residence are short. (6) Maximum areas of individual choice are to be sought, within the limits of social need and the common good. (7) The rights and obligations of minorities must be protected and nurtured, not as a concession but as a matter of natural right.

There are other items which can readily be added to the list. Any campus which freshly addresses itself to the problems of American racism while using governance processes which are designed to teach the lessons of fully operative democracy will be on the road toward campus peace. Perhaps it will be a rocky road; but it will be an open road. It will lead somewhere other than into a dead end or over the cliff.

CHAPTER IX

TOWN AND GOWN

All the problems of college and race come to sharp focus and at an intensified level of difficulty in the relationships between campus and society. The classic quandary of college presidents and deans has always been the clash of Town and Gown: but the classic problem today assumes explosive proportions because of potential racial conflict.

There is reason to doubt that society will permit education to pursue the goals of racial justice even if the will to do so were to emerge on campus. This doubt is especially strong in a time when campus change appears to come mainly in the wake of violence and disruption or the threat thereof, rather than as a result of considered and planned progress.

For example, the political campaigns which demanded "law and order" ought to be viewed not so much as venal efforts by politicians to capitalize on widespread aversions and fears, but rather as symptoms of a malaise which alienates the generations and the races from each other. And as the seat of academic authority has shifted from the college president's office to City Hall or the State Capitol (and potentially to Capitol Hill, the Pentagon and the White House), campus unrest has found off-campus targets increasingly enticing, along with those more readily assailable on campus. At the same time, the ordinary citizen who lives in a mortgaged home and pays his taxes to support the institutions of higher education is demanding that colleges force unruly students to settle down at the books and get on with the inculcation of established values. The financial crisis which currently threatens the existence of one-third of the nation's colleges and universities and erodes the quality of another third should be viewed as something more than the failure of institutional income to keep up with mounting costs. It is also a crisis of confidence—people refuse to pay for something they mistrust. Even more, it is a crisis of relevance: institutions are neglected when they become negligible.

Within these crises of confidence and relevance, an even more crucial confrontation has emerged, dividing those who defend segregation from those who seek integration. The segregationist loses confidence in higher education when institutions cease to serve his racist desires; and the integrationist loses confidence through every dragging week of delay in the elimination of racism on campus. A significant part of the answer to this dilemma might come through the effort to achieve institutional relevance to social need. The campus, if it cared enough, might reverse the trend. It might become the source of healing influences to conquer and cure the racial malaise of America. Such relevance could create confidence.

One reason that this has not happened on a wide front is found in the reluctance of many educators to pull down their own ivory towers and ivied walls and to seek the educational task as one which includes the rebuilding of society. Certainly this argument is forceful when limited solely to the question of race. All of the weight of the law, the Constitution and the courts is on the side of racial justice and brotherhood. Not to throw the efforts of the college into the struggle to attain these genuinely American goals is to refuse to be relevant to social need in a moment of rare opportunity—a moment which is fast waning and which will not recur. To miss the opportunity to be relevant in the curing of racism is to ensure that the forces of segregation and other forms of injustice will prevail, and that they will therefore necessarily prevail on campus as well as off.

White racism can be attacked, directly and with success, by any college or university which firmly wishes to do so. The schedule and rate of change may be different under varying circumstances; but the possibility of constructive change is far greater than the timid suspect. The fault lies primarily in paralysis of the will.

Not that white society will quickly and unanimously applaud the effort: quite the contrary. And that is why the town-and-gown relationship is of crucial importance. No campus can, today, over the long haul expect to be successful in maintaining the posture that it is exempt from the laws and norms of surrounding society. The only way to avoid capitulation to White Supremacy on campus lies in the effort to eradicate racism both on and off campus.

There was a time, perhaps five to ten years ago, when white racism could have been attacked with high expectations of early success and with the probable support of most blacks. That moment of opportunity was frittered away. With each passing month of inaction the chances of success decrease.

One reason for the declining hope of success is the changing character of the inner city, as whites flee to the suburbs and blacks are ghettoized. A second cause of declining expectation is the tightening of racial tensions which always accompanies economic and financial hard times. (For example, annual fluctuations in the price of cotton were always followed by inverse fluctuations in the number of lynchings in the cotton growing states, up until the economic situation was stabilized through government control of crops and prices.) A third factor which dims immediate hopes of a successful attack on white racism is the contemporary burgeoning of black racism—partly as a result of rage born of long-deferred hope, and partly because human nature is widely distributed amongst mankind.

46

The principal difficulty in overcoming white racism is fear: fear of the unknown; fear of losing dearly bought property; fear of having nobody to feel better than; fear of change; fear of rhetoric, rage and reprisal. The principal difficulty in overcoming black racism is hatred: hatred deriving from centuries of oppression and deprivation, hatred of the symbols and fact of White Supremacy, hatred of the Have-Nots toward the Haves, hatred toward a nation which never became the land of the free because it never was the home of the brave. And as white fear and black hatred, together, escalate one another through confrontation, while guns are oiled and wariness grows into vigilance, what answers are proposed?

Most frequently heard are the demands for the use of force and counter-force. "Call out the cops. Use the National Guard. Shoot 'em down!" Or, from the other side, "Burn, baby, burn. Off the pigs. Trash the place!" It makes little difference that history demonstrates that force is counter-productive, even self-defeating, settling nothing. Neither side seems to have learned the one important lesson of America's fratricidal war, namely, that the only clear verdict of that conflict was that you can't secede from the Union unless your army is strong enough. The fate of Biafra does not deter the anger of black Americans, any more than the precarious peril of white South Africa quiets the rhetoric of the Ku Klux Klan. Neither side faces the facts of history.

If there is a countervailing influence which can open up some alternative other than the use of force and counter-force, that influence ought to be present in the colleges and universities of the nation, where reason and logic and facts and humanness and compassion are supposed to be resident.

How do these qualities become part of the educational goals and achievements of the American campus? By practicing them, not merely by lecturing about them or passing resolutions in Student Senate and Faculty Council.

And that is why the relationship between college and society is of basic importance. If a campus wishes to teach the qualities of an inclusive humanity instead of unhumane exclusiveness, it must embody these qualities not only on its own campus but also in the town and city immediately surrounding it, and in ever widening circles of influence and concern. The college cannot teach justice and equity and social need while it practices racial injustice, racial inequity and two societies. Neither can the college survive in isolation from society. The campus will go down with a racist society, caught between the back-lash and the black-lash—or it will be part of a successful effort to cure the fears and quiet the hatreds which divide us as a nation.

And if there is one clear lesson to be learned from the long, stubbornly continued struggle for civil rights in America, it is this: you don't know what you can do until you've done it. There are amazing resources of the spirit and of the will resident in the minds and hearts of millions of both races, waiting to be released in a common effort to bring in the day of brotherhood and end the night of wrong. Some of it is on campus. Some of it is off campus. It is time the two got together.

The failure of separatism has been amply demonstrated. Integration has not failed. It has never been fully tried.

CHAPTER X

THE CHECK-UP

Most American campuses are committed to the goals of an Open Society; but most of them also appear to think that their responsibility ends when that commitment has been announced. Both responsibility and opportunity begin—not end—with such commitment.

To be committed, then to know the full meaning of the commitment, and then to know precisely what to do—and to be doing it, making steady progress in continuously adhering to the goals of the Open Society—this is to be relevant. The campus which achieves such relevance deserves to survive. It deserves the freedom from turbulence which it will certainly attain, if it perseveres.

Responsibility does not cease with color-blind admissions. It only begins there. What follows in this check list will, by the nature of things, be made up of different specifics of response on different campuses. Measures and procedures appropriate to each campus will have to be worked out there, and kept in constant review. Nevertheless, most of the items in the following check list will apply to most campuses.

Yes No
☐   ☐ This institution is an Affirmative Action Equal Opportunity Employer.

☐   ☐ Our declared policy is that no person shall, on the basis of race, color, or national origin, be excluded from participation in, be denied the benefits of, or subjected to discrimination under, any program or activity.

☐   ☐ We have devised methods and procedures for converting declared policy into effective daily processes, at every level of authority and responsibility and throughout the formal and informal life of the institution.

☐   ☐ These methods and procedures work.

☐   ☐ In the administration, the faculties and the student body, there is effective and substantial leadership which is engaged in continuous reexamination of priorities and procedures in the light of changing situations and with a view to working toward equality in an open society.

☐   ☐ These responsible leaders each know what the other is doing; they talk to each other and work together.

49

Yes	No
☐	☐ All segments of the academic community can—and do—make an in-put in matters of policy decision.
☐	☐ We recruit students—actively recruit them—so as to insure a multi-racial student body. We have a multi-racial student body, and we don't settle for "tokenism."
☐	☐ Support services and supplementary help—financial, educational, psychological—are available for those who need them. Financial aid is adequate; corrective educational help speedily gets students into the mainstream of college work; and psychological counselling gets to the student early enough to be of use.
☐	☐ Both the administration and the faculty personnel include more than token representation of minority groups at levels of real responsibility. Race is never a disqualifying factor in appointment or promotion, in any position.
☐	☐ Both the curriculum and extra-curricular life draw on, and present affirmatively, the culture and history of all races without distortion or omissions.
☐	☐ Housing, health, food and recreation facilities and services are provided without segregation or other form of discrimination, and also in varieties of taste and preference which respect the wishes of all, on an open-access basis.
☐	☐ Our honor societies and social fraternities and sororities do not have restrictive clauses in their constitutions and do have membership which is multi-racial. There are no exceptions.
☐	☐ We have an effective process for hearing grievances and correcting inequities. It works.
☐	☐ Our campus society is generally open and receptive, There is a readiness to listen as well as to talk, and a willingness to adapt and to change. Forums for debate and discussion, as well as for deliberation and decision, are free and open. Participants are not inhibited, threatened or otherwise prevented from speaking their minds freely and without reprisal.
☐	☐ Our campus governance is democratic. It works.
☐	☐ We have an ombudsman and he is effective.
☐	☐ Local and state government officials know the plans and goals of this college in achieving an Open Society; and on campus there is clear knowledge of the extent to which each official can be relied upon to support equal educa-

tion and the opportunity to be equal—and what he is likely to do in a crisis.

☐   ☐ The objectives of the institution are clearly understood by all members of the governing board, administration, faculty, student body, alumni association, custodial and administrative staffs, and parents of present and future students. There is a continuous effort to keep everybody informed, plus periodic planned communication. The communication is two-way.

☐   ☐ Both the campus and the surrounding community have been prepared to accept varieties in dress, language, taste and social customs; but this preparation is nevertheless a continuous recurring conscious effort.

☐   ☐ Members of minorities, newly arriving on campus, are prepared to understand prevailing values and customs of campus and community.

☐   ☐ Every individual on campus has ready access to a religious institution which is congenial to him: busing where necessary.

☐   ☐ We on campus are in close touch with local off-campus resources such as the local Youth Council or Branch of the NAACP.

☐   ☐ There is an annual check-up and public report on problems and progress in the ethnic area. I have read such a report.

☐   ☐ During the past week, I have made a significant contribution to decency, justice, equality and affirmative affection between the races.

☐   ☐ I have read all of this tract; and I am now personally putting it into the hands of another who will promise to do the same.

On the campus where it had been thought that the announcement of color-blind admissions would discharge all obligations, the foregoing check list may help to widen the scope of matters to be considered. None should assume, however, that an affirmative answer to every item would indicate a campus which had attained perfection. The list is suggestive, not exhaustive, as a perusal of the appended Cincinnati Statement will show.

The job which waits to be done is large enough and pressing enough to make institutional self-congratulation inappropriate, perhaps egregious.

If a significant number of items in the check list are answered negatively, it may be assumed that the institution either is now in deep trouble or soon will be.

APPENDIX

THE NAACP SPEAKS TO THE TROUBLED CAMPUS

(Adopted unanimously by the National Board of Directors of the NAACP, Cincinnati, Ohio, July 2, 1970.)

In the face of mounting fears and hatreds, not infrequently climaxed in violence and death, the NAACP has, with particular vehemence over the last four years, warned that separation and segregation lead inexorably to further division and hatred. The one right road is total commitment to one society—integrated and equal. Our sixty-one-year struggle to attain this goal has known many dangerous times—few more perilous than today's—and we do not intend to lose that struggle now.

Of special importance in this critical hour is the matter of integration and equality in the nation's colleges and universities—both the existing institutions and those which are about to be founded to meet the population explosion in the decade immediately ahead. We direct our attention to the campuses both of the so-called predominantly black and the so-called predominantly white institutions, with equal concern for the welfare of students in both, and with an expression of dismay over the growth of separatism and the flourishing of segregation in both.

We do not propose to waste energy in an escalation of rhetoric. In this statement, we address ourselves constructively to the nation's campuses and call for concerted action, without which the polarization of higher education will become a principal source of further division, separation, segregation and violence in the nation.

With the National Commission on the Causes and Prevention of Violence, we agree

"that most of this violence can be prevented. . . . Our institutions and the spirit of our people are equal to this challenge. . . . Responsible participation in decision-making may, for many, be a substitute for the violence that is born of frustration. . . .

"While we categorically condemn all illegal violence, including group violence, as incompatible with the survival of a just, democratic, and humane society, we state emphatically that aggrieved groups must be permitted to exercise their constitutional rights of protest and public presentation of grievances. . . .

"The way in which we can make the greatest progress toward reducing violence in America is by taking the actions necessary to improve the conditions of family and community life for all who live in our cities, and especially for the poor who are concentrated in the ghetto slums. . . .

"In our judgment, the time is upon us for reordering of national priorities and for a greater investment of our resources in the fulfillment of two basic purposes of our Constitution—to 'establish justice' and to 'insure domestic tranquility.' "

I

Addressing ourselves to all existing institutions of higher education, we commend the following lines of commitment for immediate and full acceptance and for immediate and sustained action:

A. *Equal opportunity:*
1. Open admission which strikes down all barriers of race, creed, national origin, and ability to pay; accompanied by
2. Necessary compensatory and supporting services which prevent the open door from becoming a revolving door for the poor and the under-prepared; within the framework of
3. A greater diversity of types of higher education and of courses of professional and cultural studies.

B. *Non-segregated colleges and universities:*
1. Integrated dormitories and living and eating facilities, without exception; together with
2. Integrated (open admissions to) curricula and courses of study, without exception; implemented by
3. Active recruitment of students from the inner city; made effective by
4. Concerted and continuing attention to the special needs of each student—including but not limited to—the needs arising from minority group status in a pluralistic society (such as the need for instruction to begin where a student is rather than where the syllabus says he ought to be, and the need for compensatory and supporting services to make real his opportunity to be equal).
5. Among other things, the time has come to make the push for integrated student bodies and faculties at the campuses of the so-called predominantly Negro colleges and universities, while not relenting the pressure for integration of the so-called predominantly white institutions.

C. *Higher Education relevant to individual and social needs:*
1. The problems and needs of an urban society, and especially the economics, sociology and political science of the inner city and the ghetto slum, as a central emphasis of curricular offerings and study; together with

2. The full recognition of the history and culture of all minorities as a part of the history and heritage of all Americans (calling for special but non-segregated courses of study as the initial step in correcting—in most instances—the blindness, ignorance or prejudices and indifference of most curricular planners up to the very recent past).

D. *The democratized college and university:*
   1. Through elected representation, the sharing of students, faculty and administrators in the making of campus policy and the governance of each institution—without adequate safeguards of minority rights and interests;
   2. The democratizing of boards of control through the inclusion of representatives from economic classes and racial groups too often disregarded in constituting the board of control; and
   3. The determined recruitment of administrators and teachers from racial groups and economic classes of national, cultural and religious backgrounds commonly overlooked, an objective which demands, in most instances, a re-examination not only of institutional policy and practice, but also of the processes and criteria of certification and credentials;
   4. The speeding-up of the decision-making process so that frustration is replaced by achievement; and
   5. The full and careful safeguarding of the rights of free speech, free association and free assembly (including non-violent protest and demonstration), for every student, teacher and administrator, regardless of race, creed or national origin.

II

Addressing ourselves to the need for new institutions of higher education, we cite the fact that more than five hundred *new* colleges and universities will be needed within the next two decades (about half by 1980) if the children already born are to have educational opportunities equal even to the restricted openings of 1970.

The founding of these new institutions affords an unparalled opportunity to avoid the errors of the past and to begin aggressively to meet the needs of late twentieth century America. By the year 2000, about eighty-five percent of the population will live in urban centers. Higher education must direct its attention to the quality of life in the urban sprawl, ministering to the needs of an urban society and the people in it.

The Land Grant University was a new type of institution, founded by a far-seeing Federal Government in the final quarter of the nineteenth century, primarily to meet the needs of the rural countryside—

where most of the population then lived. It was, in reality, the first great anti-poverty program of this nation.

The plight of the cities and especially of the dweller in the inner city today makes it imperative that a series of *"Urban Grant Universities"* be speedily established and nurtured. Drawing on the experience of the Land Grant University (both the successes, the partial successes, and the failures), the Urban Grant University should:

1. Be fully integrated in all aspects, without exception;
2. Be fully open to all, without exception;
3. Curricularize the learning experience of the city-dweller (as the Land Grant University curricularized farm life);
4. Through on-campus offerings and informal instruction and through off-campus extension of educational and other services, provide the urban equivalent of the Land Grant University's "short course," the Agricultural Experiment Station, the County Agent, the 4-H Clubs, etc.;
5. Through the composition and structuring of its board of control, its educational and administrative policy and practice, and its educative experiences, foreshadow the integrated society of free men which it seeks to create.

This new university will be oriented not primarily toward the historic academic disciplines but toward the problems of an urban society and the solution thereof.

Being mission-and-problem-oriented, the Urban Grant University will utilize only those structures and processes of the contemporary college and university which are clearly useful to its mission and clearly helpful in mastering the problems of the city and the city-dweller— among which problems are poverty, disease, violence (including war), racism, and the threat of anti-democratic forces.

The Urban Grant University will be funded primarily by Federal initiative and support, as were the Land Grant Universities at their beginnings. State and municipal resources will be an important, though lesser, part of the financing.

The new universities will be located where the people are—primarily in the inner city.

Wherever useful, the new university will be guided by the check list recited in Part I of this statement. It will not repeat the errors of separatism, segregation and irrelevance.

The legislation to establish these new universities should be a matter of immediate concern in the Congress and in the Executive Branch of the Federal Government.

III

In addition to the matters discussed in Parts I and II of this statement, the NAACP calls urgent attention to the following:

55

The full answer to violence and disruption on campus cannot come from repression and the counter-productive use of military and police forces, but from the correction of the basic causes of student unrest (among which poverty, disease, violence—including war—racism and the threat of repressive reaction must be included in any list, however short) and the re-structuring of academic life and institutions so that the student and professor are actually sharing in shaping their own destiny rather than being forced through frustration and bitterness to resort to fantasies of revolution and the actualities of rebellion.

In short, a total commitment to one society, integrated and equal, means that universities and the society which supports them must be fully integrated, unhampered by prejudice, free of the threat of re-pression and violence from within or without, open to constructive growth, and rooted in the urban communities they serve.

Respectfully submitted,
/s/   James Blake
Kenneth R. Brown *
Silas E. Craft
Carl C. McCraven
Jahue Nash, Jr.*
Evelyn H. Roberts
Daniel W. Wright III *
Buell G. Gallagher, Chairman

Cincinnati, Ohio
June 28, 1970

* Youth Members.